Social Issues
in Literature

| Race in John Howard
Griffin's *Black Like Me*

Other Books in the Social Issues in Literature Series:

Social Issues
in Literature

Race in John Howard Griffin's *Black Like Me*

David E. Nelson, Book Editor

GREENHAVEN PRESS
A part of Gale, Cengage Learning

GALE
CENGAGE Learning

Detroit • New York • San Francisco • New Haven, Conn • Waterville, Maine • London

Elizabeth Des Chenes, *Director, Publishing Solutions*

© 2013 Greenhaven Press, a part of Gale, Cengage Learning

Gale and Greenhaven Press are registered trademarks used herein under license.

For more information, contact:
Greenhaven Press
27500 Drake Rd.
Farmington Hills, MI 48331-3535
Or you can visit our Internet site at gale.cengage.com

For product information and technology assistance, contact us at

Gale Customer Support, 1-800-877-4253
For permission to use material from this text or product, submit all requests online at
www.cengage.com/permissions

Further permissions questions can be emailed to permissionrequest@cengage.com

Articles in Greenhaven Press anthologies are often edited for length to meet page requirements. In addition, original titles of these works are changed to clearly present the main
thesis and to explicitly indicate the author's opinion. Every effort is made to ensure that
Greenhaven Press accurately reflects the original intent of the authors. Every effort has
been made to trace the owners of copyrighted material.

Cover image © Bettmann/Corbis.

LIBRARY OF CONGRESS CATALOGING-IN-PUBLICATION DATA

Race in John Howard Griffith's Black like me / David E. Nelson, book editor.
    p. cm. -- (Social issues in literature)
Includes bibliographical references and index.
    ISBN 978-0-7377-6373-7 (hardcover) -- ISBN 978-0-7377-6374-4 (pbk.)
1. Griffin, John Howard, 1920-1980. Black like me. 2. Race in literature. 3. African Americans--Southern States--Social conditions. 4. Southern States--Race relations. 5. Nelson, David E.
    PS3557.R489Z84 2013
    814'.54--dc23

                                                                        2012036367

Printed in Mexico
1 2 3 4 5 6 7 16 15 14 13 12

Contents

Chapter 3: Contemporary Perspectives on Race

Introduction

John Howard Griffin led an extraordinary life. Many of the circumstances of his life—including the sea change taking place in American race relations at the time—informed his experiment in "passing" as a black man, an experiment he wrote about in the book for which he is best known, *Black Like Me*. Griffin was born in Dallas, Texas, in 1920. Although his family and friends thought of themselves as "good whites" who treated all people fairly, Griffin's community was far from immune to the assumptions of racial superiority that permeated the United States at that time.

In 1935 fifteen-year-old Griffin was hungry for a "classical" education. He secured a scholarship to study at the Lycée Descartes in Tours, France, despite speaking no French. There Griffin discovered his own previously invisible racism: Despite his view of himself as fair-minded, he was distressed to be seated in the same dining hall, using the same facilities, and treated as no better or worse than his dark-skinned classmates.

Griffin completed his studies at the Lycée and went on to attend the University of Poitiers, where he studied music (his mother was a classical pianist), and the École de Médecine, where he studied medicine, largely focusing on the new field of psychology. While at the École de Médecine, Griffin interned at the Asylum of Tours, where he experimented with using music in the treatment of the "criminally insane."

In 1939, as Nazi Germany attacked and conquered ever greater swaths of Europe, many American expatriates returned to the safety of US soil. Griffin, by contrast, stayed in France and served in the French Resistance as a medic. He conspired to help dozens of Jewish children flee to England to escape Nazi persecution and certain death. When the French Resistance learned that this work had landed Griffin on a list of "agents" sought by the German Gestapo (secret police), Griffin's comrades smuggled him out of France as well.

On returning to the United States, Griffin enlisted in the US Army Air Corps (the forerunner of the US Air Force). While serving in the air corps, Griffin was stationed on the small South Pacific island of Nuni for more than two years. These tiny islands were of great strategic importance in the Pacific theater of World War II against imperial Japan, so US forces sought to build good relationships with the islanders. Griffin's role on Nuni was largely sociological and diplomatic, as a sort of goodwill ambassador. He was the only American stationed there, and subsequently the only white person. When he arrived there, he shared no language or common culture with his hosts.

In 1944 Griffin was injured during a Japanese bombing raid against the radio post he manned. He suffered neurological damage that caused his vision to deteriorate, and by 1947 he was completely blind. Griffin traveled back to France, where he continued his music studies at the Conservatory of Fontainebleau in the Abbey of Solesmes. By 1952 he had returned to Texas, where he gave piano lessons for a living and married Elizabeth Anne Holland. Five years later, likely as a side effect of medicine he was taking to treat a lingering case of malaria he had contracted while stationed on Nuni, Griffin regained his vision. For the first time he saw his wife and children.

As a blind man, Griffin had made three important discoveries. First and foremost was the pain of being constantly and incorrectly judged as incompetent or helpless, regardless of how capable he demonstrated himself to be. Second was his realization that he really could *not* identify race when he could no longer see a person's skin. And finally, he found that when people no longer thought they were being judged based on their appearance, they were able to be much more honest about how they felt and how they saw the world.

Griffin's experience with blindness significantly informed his decision to embark on his famous race experiment in 1959, resulting in his 1961 memoir *Black Like Me*. Although this book was initially well received by African American readers and reviewers, *Black Like Me* was widely criticized by black intellectuals later in the 1960s and throughout the 1970s. Malcolm X dismissed Griffin's work, noting: "If it was a frightening experience for him as nothing but a make-believe Negro for 66 days, then you think about what real Negroes in America have gone through for 400 years." Activist Stokely Carmichael, most notable for his early influence on the Black Panthers and for coining the phrase "Black Power," famously quipped that *Black Like Me* "is an excellent book—for whites."

Griffin did not dispute this. Writing a "book for whites" was implicitly his goal from the start, and he stated that goal as early as 1963. After all, he hardly needed to tell African Americans what it was like to live in America, but many basically good-hearted white Americans still permitted themselves to believe that things were not really so bad for blacks.

By the time Griffin died in 1980 his book had become something of a curiosity. The 1960s fight for equality had evolved into a much more subtle struggle for educational and economic opportunities, and America had—much like the young Griffin in France—finally acknowledged its own racism. More often than not *Black Like Me* was dismissed unread—the persistence of racial inequality was no longer a terrible revelation.

Black Like Me has, however, enjoyed a recent resurgence among African American thinkers and educators. It has also found a new audience among post–civil-rights-era students, many of whom are surprised by the extent of the racial hatred and inequality depicted in Griffin's book—and surprised to realize the extent to which discrimination persists today.

Chronology

1920

John Howard Griffin is born on June 16 in Dallas, Texas, to John Walter Griffin and Lena May Young Griffin, a classical pianist.

1935

Griffin moves to France to study at the Lycée Descartes in Tours, where he completes high school.

1938–1939

Griffin attends the University of Poitiers (studying music) and L'école de Médecine (studying medicine).

1939

Griffin leaves his studies to join the French Resistance, serving as a medic and helping Jews flee Nazi persecution.

1942

Griffin Joins the US Army Air Corps (the forerunner to the US Air Force).

1943–1944

Griffin is stationed on the island of Nuni in the Solomon Islands, where he is the only Caucasian.

1944

Griffin is injured in a Japanese bombing raid, causing his vision to begin to deteriorate. By 1947 he is completely blind.

1947

Griffin studies piano at the Conservatory of Fontainebleau, Abbey of Solesmes, in France.

1952

Griffin returns to Texas, converts to Catholicism, begins teaching piano, and marries Elizabeth Anne Holland.

1952

Griffin publishes his first novel, *The Devil Rides Outside*.

1956

Griffin publishes his second novel, *Nuni*, largely based on his time on the island of that name.

1957

Griffin gradually regains his sight after more than a decade of blindness. He sees his wife and two children for the first time. He begins acclaimed work as a photographer and chronicles his period of blindness in the collection of essays *Scattered Shadows: A Memoir of Blindness and Vision* (published posthumously in 2004).

1959

Griffin performs his famous experiment in racial passing, dying his skin dark and traveling throughout the American South as an African American. He documents this in a series of articles for *Sepia* magazine (an African American publication) under the title "Journey into Shame."

1961

Griffin publishes *Black Like Me*; he begins to tour extensively, talking about the experiences on which *Black Like Me* is based and working in the civil rights movement.

1962

Griffin meets the noted American Trappist monk Thomas Merton (1915–1968). He will spend the latter half of his life researching Merton and his works.

1964

Griffin is assaulted and brutally beaten by members of the Ku Klux Klan, the first of several times he is physically assaulted on account of his book.

1969

Griffin publishes *The Church and the Black Man.*

1980

Griffin dies on September 9 of complications from diabetes.

1983

Griffin's authorized biography of Merton, *Follow the Ecstasy: Thomas Merton, the Hermitage Years, 1965–1968*, his last great work, is published posthumously.

CHAPTER 1

Background on John Howard Griffin

The Life of
John Howard Griffin

Contemporary Literary Criticism

Contemporary Literary Criticism is a multivolume series of anthologies of full-text or excerpted criticism of today's authors taken from books, magazines, literary reviews, newspapers, and scholarly journals.

*The following selection offers a brief overview of John Howard Griffin's early life, education, and writing career, paying special attention to the impact Griffin's military service and years of blindness had on his professional and spiritual growth. The authors note Griffin's most significant novels (*The Devil Rides Outside *and* Nuni*), as well as his most important nonfiction works. The authors describe the controversy that followed the publication of Griffin's best-known work,* Black Like Me, *noting that its frank depiction of a racist society "struck a nerve" with many readers.*

[J]ohn Howard] Griffin's work is predominantly concerned with humanity's spiritual well-being as determined by social and personal growth. For example, his first novel, *The Devil Rides Outside*, examines both monastic and secular lifestyles as encountered by a young man obsessed with physical pleasure, divine grace, and spiritual salvation. His next novel, *Nuni*, is an anthropological account of a Westerner stranded on a South Pacific island whose inhabitants consider Western expressions of love and affection *zagata*, or "no good." Griffin's belief in humanity's potential for reform led to his active participation in the American civil rights movement during the 1960s. His most famous book, *Black Like Me*, chronicles the racism he encountered in the South when he disguised himself as a black man. The controversial subject matter of his works catapulted Griffin into the role of social commentator, combating what he called the "very worst development of recent years . . . that people no longer feel a sense of horror (or even *uneasiness*) in the face of injustice that simply wrecks human lives."

Education and Military Service

Griffin was born in Dallas, Texas. While in his teens, he attended the Lycée Descartes in Tours, France, where he studied science, music, and philosophy. After graduation, Griffin studied psychiatry at the École de Médecine de Tours. Despite his decision to pursue a career in medicine, Griffin continued his musical studies. He collaborated on a book about the early modern music of the Roman Catholic church and combined his love for music and medical science by prescribing music therapy for his patients. When World War II broke out, Griffin was placed in a supervisory position at the Asylum of Tours, became active in the French Resistance, and helped many Jews escape Nazi persecution by loading them on ambulances under the pretense that they were patients being transferred to other facilities. When France fell to Germany in 1940, Griffin returned to the United States and enlisted in the Air Force, serving in the Pacific, first on the island of Nuni and then on Morotai as a liaison between the islanders and American forces. During an air raid on Morotai, he sustained head injuries that left him legally blind and received a medical discharge. After the war ended, Griffin returned to France to study music with Nadia Boulanger—an acclaimed conductor, lecturer, and teacher of music composition. While researching the origins of the Gregorian chant, a melody used in Roman Catholic liturgies, he visited the Couvent St. Jacques as well as the Benedictine Abbey of Solesmes, where he became familiar

John Howard Griffin, author of Black Like Me, *in 1960.* © Ben Martin/Time & Life Pictures/Getty Images.

with the teachings of Roman Catholicism. These experiences led to Griffin's conversion and provided the basis for *The Devil Rides Outside.*

Blindness, Writing, and Civil Rights

After Griffin completely lost his sight in 1947, he returned to the United States to attend schools for the blind and to study philosophy with Jacques Maritain, of whom he later wrote a biography. He eventually settled on his parents' farm in Mansfield, Texas, and took up cattle-breeding, teaching piano, and creative writing. By dictating his work into a wire recorder, Griffin was able to compose *The Devil Rides Outside* and *Nuni*. During this time, Griffin also began taking strychnine to treat a case of malaria which had left him partially paralyzed. An unexpected side effect of the drug restored circulation to blood vessels in Griffin's eyes and allowed him to regain his vision. In 1959 he suggested to the editors of *Sepia*, a magazine directed at a black audience, that he research a story on the treatment of the black person in the American South. In order to experience the hardships suffered by his subjects, Griffin affected the appearance of a black man using sun lamps, vegetable dyes, and pigment-enhancing drugs. His experiences were reported in *Sepia*'s "Journey into Shame" series and were later published as *Black Like Me*. Griffin's reproach of southern white society prompted hostility in his community, and, in order to escape harassment, he and his family fled to Mexico. Upon his return to Texas in 1961, Griffin abandoned writing projects that were near completion and began lecturing on civil rights. Prior to the 1969 publication of *The Church and the Black Man*, which called for the Catholic church to become more actively involved in the civil rights movement, he befriended and worked with Trappist monk and author Thomas Merton. Between 1968 and 1971, Griffin made frequent trips to Gethsemani Abbey in Kentucky, where he visited Merton and made numerous spiritual retreats, eventually earning a commission from the Merton Legacy to write Merton's biography. Poor health prevented Griffin from meeting deadlines for the book, however, and permission was revoked in 1978. Griffin died in 1980, but the journals he kept while working on the biography were published a year later as *The Hermitage Journals*.

Griffin's Two Novels

Griffin's first novel, *The Devil Rides Outside*, chronicles a young man's struggle for spiritual salvation. While studying at a monastery, the narrator longs for the mystical spirituality and inner peace that the monks have achieved, and strives to imitate their lifestyle by curbing his own carnal desires. While the work was praised for its accurate descriptions of monastic life and its confessional honesty, critics thought the novel overlong, unorganized, and marred by extended philosophical digressions which were often disguised as speeches. Griffin also faced opposition from the Legion for Decent Literature, which took offense at graphic descriptions of the characters' sexual urges and encounters; these passages became the basis for lawsuits that the state of Michigan brought against the book's distributors. Eventually the case was brought before the United States Supreme Court, which ruled in the distributors' favor.

Like *The Devil Rides Outside*, *Nuni* is largely autobiographical. This novel stems from Griffin's experiences in the South Pacific during World War II and his observations of the islanders' culture. In *Nuni*, the protagonist learns the language, legends, rites, and norms of the natives and attempts to instill Western values in them. While critics found Griffin's stream-of-consciousness technique and use of the present tense confusing, they also recognized the novel's importance as a sociological account of life among the Pacific aborigines. Some commentators also argued that *Nuni* might have been more effective if presented as an anthropological study rather than as a piece of fiction.

Black Like Me

Black Like Me is Griffin's most famous and controversial book. In this work, Griffin describes his travels in New Orleans, Mississippi, Alabama, and Georgia, during which the simplest tasks of obtaining food and lodging became obstacles. Under the Jim Crow laws, blacks were treated as second-class citizens who were often legally prevented from voting; restricted to the "colored" sections of towns, restaurants, trains, and buses; and denied employment and entrance to social institutions and educational facilities. More devastating and humiliating, however, was the way in which Griffin was treated by the white people he encountered. Frank London Brown notes that Griffin now "met the 'hate stare' ['I walked up to the ticket counter. When the lady ticket seller saw me, her otherwise attractive face turned sour, violently so.']; he met neurosis in depth ['I understand you make more of an art—or maybe *hobby*—out of your sex than we do.']; he met despair ['Suddenly I had had enough. Suddenly I could stomach no more of this degradation—not of myself but of all men who were black like me.']" The descriptions of life in a racist society struck a nerve in many Americans, and most negative criticism came from the reading public. As a result, Griffin was hanged in effigy, denounced, and often banned from speaking in public. Literary critics praised the book as an example of the New Journalism movement, citing the author's participation in the story; yet others found the work unbalanced and wanted either more emphasis placed on everyday experiences faced by black men and women, or more examples of Griffin's own experiences and fewer philosophical digressions. Despite claims that the book belittled both black and white cultures, *Black Like Me* received praise for its honesty and emotional impact, and became the basis for a motion picture in 1964.

Rumors Persist That Griffin Died of Skin Cancer

Barbara Mikkelson and David P. Mikkelson

Barbara Mikkelson and David P. Mikkelson have operated the Snopes.com website since 1995. Their site is widely regarded by journalists, folklorists, and other researchers as the premier website for exploring and debunking popular myths.

In the following article, Barbara and David P. Mikkelson address the popular myth that John Howard Griffin died of skin cancer as a direct consequence of his chemically aided experiment in racial passing. Beyond dispensing with this simple inaccuracy— Griffin did not die of skin cancer at all, but rather as a consequence of diabetes and heart disease—the authors also offer insights into the source of this rumor and why it has persisted, despite being so easily disproven.

Claim: John Howard Griffin, the author of *Black Like Me*, died from skin cancer caused by the treatment he underwent to darken his skin.

FALSE

Griffin's Real-Life Challenges

Origins: John Howard Griffin was born in Dallas, Texas, in 1920 but left the United States for France at age fifteen in pursuit of a classical education. While barely out of his teens, he had completed studies in such diverse fields as French, literature, medicine, and music, worked as an intern conducting experiments in the use of music as therapy for the criminally insane, specialized in medieval music under the Benedictines at the Abbey of Solesmes, and was contemplating making the religious life his vocation. He wrote about his experiences at the Abbey and the personal struggles he underwent during this period of his life in his 1952 book, *The Devil Rides Outside*.

The outbreak of World War II intruded upon Griffin's plans; he responded to the challenge by calling upon his medical training to serve as a medic in France before spending three years with the U.S. Army Air Corps in the South Seas (where he was decorated for bravery). During Griffin's military service a head injury caused by an exploding shell caused his eyesight to deteriorate to the point that he eventually went completely blind. Nonetheless, he continued writing and turned out several novels before his eyesight miraculously returned in 1957; he later chronicled this dark period of his life in an unpublished work entitled *Scattered Shadows*.

Griffin's best-known struggle against adversity, however was a self-imposed one: In 1959, after shaving his head and using drugs and ultraviolet light to darken his skin, Griffin spent six weeks traveling through the states of Louisiana, Mississippi, Alabama, and Georgia posing as an itinerant black man in order to record a firsthand account of the virulent racism still prevalent in the Deep South. Griffin's account of his experiences, published as the book *Black Like Me* in 1961, is a gripping tale of degradation and cruelty, an account of a man who becomes the target of rudeness, indignities, insults, racial slurs, and violent threats, and is denied the basic necessities of life—a place to live, work, transportation, even the use of restrooms—simply because his skin is dark. Particularly revealing experiences came at the end of Griffin's investigation when he switched back and forth between his black and white identities and observed the negative reactions he received from people (both black and white) who had treated him kindly just days, or even hours, earlier.

Black Like Me *author John Howard Griffin in 1963.* © Bettmann/Corbis.

The Foundation of the Myth

Even well before Griffin's death in 1980, rumors began circulating that he had died as a direct result of his *Black Like Me* experiment: the treatments he undertook to darken his skin, people whispered, had led to his contracting an ultimately fatal case of skin cancer. As the authors of *Rumor!* [Hal Morgan and Kerry Tucker] noted:

> Since many people deeply resented Griffin's book and the racial tensions it exposed—he and his family moved to Mexico for a time after he was hanged in effigy in his hometown of Mansfield, Texas—the rumor has an element of the sinister to it, a satisfied wish for revenge. Since many people who told the story had no quarrel with Griffin or his discoveries, the rumor doubled as a sort of ironic tragedy, showing that those who do good are not exempt from life's cruelties.

The rumors had no substance, however. Although Griffin's transformation did involve his submitting to medical treatments which posed potential health risks, he was carefully monitored by his doctor and suffered nothing more serious or lasting than temporary, relatively minor side effects [as reported by Robert Bonazzi in *Man in the Mirror*]:

> Under the direction of a New Orleans dermatologist, Griffin had taken medication orally and had exposed his entire body to the ultraviolet rays of a sun lamp. For about a week, up to fifteen hours each day, he had stretched out on a couch under the glare of the lamp. His eyes had been protected by cotton pads when he faced the lamp, and he had worn sunglasses when turned away from its rays.

> The doctor had prescribed Oxsoralen—a drug used to treat vitiligo, a cutaneous infection most common among but not exclusive to black people, which produces white splotches on the skin. Typically the medication is given over a period of six to twelve weeks. However, Griffin's experiment necessi-

tated an accelerated pace. By taking larger than normal doses of the drug along with extended exposure under the lamp, the slow darkening process was intensified.

Despite the serious health hazards, the doctor agreed to the acceleration but monitored the experiment with regular blood tests that charted any damage to the liver. None of the blood tests indicated liver damage from the Oxsoralen and, except for lassitude and extreme nausea, Griffin experienced no lasting ill-effects.

Griffin's Actual Cause of Death

Griffin did not die of skin cancer, nor did he die from any malady related to his *Black Like Me* experiment. He was in poor health for much of his adult life, not only because of the head injury he suffered in World War II but also from spinal malaria (which left him paralyzed for a time), diabetes, and osteomyelitis (an acute and chronic bone infection). Griffin's health took a serious turn for the worse when he suffered a severe heart attack while on an extended lecture tour in late 1976, yet he lived for another four years, enduring several more heart attacks and surgeries before passing away at age 60 from diabetes-related complications on 9 September 1980.

CHAPTER 2

Black Like Me and Race

Griffin Successfully Demonstrates the Ignorance and Hurtfulness of Racial Stereotypes

Robert Bonazzi

Robert Bonazzi is an essayist, poet, and fiction writer who lives in San Antonio, Texas. He is also John Howard Griffin's biographer and the literary executor of his estate.

After Griffin's experience living as an African American, he often referred to himself as an "ex-black man" or "former Negro"— much to the consternation of some critics and pundits, both black and white, who questioned the authenticity of Griffin's experience. These critics either downplayed Griffin's trauma (arguing that he could "switch back" at any time, and thus wasn't really experiencing the racism felt by African Americans) or argued that his experience was more traumatic than that of an actual African American since he, as a white man, was "not acclimated" to such daily treatment. In the following excerpt from his biography of Griffin, Bonazzi argues that Griffin's own account and writings amply argue for the universality of human experience. He explains that Griffin's experiences had a significant impact on his life and his understanding of the African American experience and that Griffin effectively conveyed that understanding to others throughout his career.

Griffin realized that skin color alone could not magically open a door to the deeper recesses of black reality. However, having experienced the journey at the human level—

rather than merely at the political or sociological levels—he believed that his suffering from the effects of racism, however brief in duration, was exactly like that of black people in all its human essentials. He continued to lecture and to characterize his experience as "when I was a Negro," and, a few years later, to call himself an "ex-black man." He considered these issues secondary. The important thing was to communicate the reality of white racism and its discrimination of black people on the basis of color. This public position was integral to reaching a large audience that tended to be white, educated, and of the middle or upper economic classes; and, since 70 percent of his listeners were students, they had some training in dialogue. Thus, he began to reach the ears of fair-minded whites in a way that opened a new bridge of dialogue between the black voices he had heard and the white community.

Fraternal Dialogue vs. Simple Monologue

His Deep South journey had confirmed what he had learned during the Mansfield school desegregation crisis, and this was further confirmed by his travels in the North. "My long stays in the inner cities convinced me again that this was a land with two groups of people possessing two entirely different sets of information and experience. The majority did not know, had no idea, what was going on in the minority communities. They viewed everything from the outside and from their own perspective." Griffin brought whites a new perspective, and the student population responded more openly than did the older white audiences. He found that the younger whites were courageous enough to listen, to really listen to a different view in the spirit of honest disagreement and thoughtful reflection.

Griffin communicated the simple truth of fraternal dialogue—that monologues merely separate, that only dialogue can unite; that monologues are deafened by their own cacophony of contradictions, while dialogue harmonized the common connections; that monologues prompted blame and denial, but dialogue awakened healthy self-criticism.

Naturally, most of his lectures were attended by black people as well as whites, and the university audiences usually included a larger proportion of black students and professors than did his church and civic lectures. Increasingly, blacks would approach him after a lecture to say that what they had heard sounded as if "a black man were speaking out of a white man's mouth." His response was to say that he preferred to be thought of as "simply a human being," and to remind them that he was *not* a spokesman for black people or anyone else except himself.

The Fundamental Ignorance of Bigotry

"Whites have sometimes argued that I felt this degradation more deeply than black people because it was new to me, whereas black people had known nothing else all their lives." He believed this argument to be based not on real experience but on one's projection of stereotypes. "This is utterly untrue," Griffin declared, for prejudice "burns any man, and no person ever gets accustomed to it that it does not burn." It had burned all the black people he had observed, spoken with, or befriended. And just as he had seen what racism did to black people, he had seen what anti-Semitism had done to the Jews during World War II. Of course, having merely witnessed what had happened in Europe when he was a young man had not affected him as profoundly as what he had experienced with his change of skin color. "Such whites say it the way they have *seen* it," he clarified in contrast to the fact that "I say it in the way I have *experienced* it."

He observed a similar pattern in all prejudice, whether racism or anti-Semitism, the superior attitude of the sighted toward him during his sightlessness, or even in the censors who had branded his work as pornographic or communist-inspired. It had always been the pattern of the ignorant con-

Movie poster for the 1964 film adaptation of Black Like Me. © John D. Kisch/Separate Cinema Archive/Getty Images.

demning anyone or any group because it did not match the so-called norm of the majority. In terms of white racism, he argued that "I can explain why they can say that"—that blacks are intrinsically different and inferior—"and why I can say I never met a black who fit the stereotype insofar as authentic ethnic characteristics are concerned. White people have always said: 'We'll treat black people right as long as they stay in their place.' But if you pinned whites down on this point, most could not say what that 'place' is, but every black person knows—it is squarely in the middle of the stereotype. Whites created the stereotype to justify their racism and then forced black people to act out the stereotype."

Bigotry Breeds Confusion and Alienation

Before the *Black Like Me* experience, Griffin held many of the same stereotypes to be true without questioning their inherent logical fallacies, believing blacks "led essentially the same kind of lives we whites know, with certain inconveniences caused by discrimination and prejudice." His deepest shock came with the gradual realization that it was not a matter of inconvenience but rather a matter of a total change in living. "Everything is different. Everything changes. As soon as I got into areas where I had contact with white people I realized that I was no longer regarded as a human individual. In our experiences as whites, whenever we meet a stranger, an aura of mystery exists between us until the stranger discovers what kind of a person we are and until we discover what kind of a person that stranger is." One's sense of a stranger in this instance—the scene of two white people meeting—suggests the possibility of discovery, for the unknown is not threatening or alien but a matter of casual socialization.

However, "when a person is imprisoned in the stereotype others hold of him, that aura of mystery is wiped away," and a simple encounter becomes fraught with tension. Instead of a white person perceiving a black person merely as a person, "all of white society looked at black people, saw the pigment, and immediately attributed to all the characteristics of the stereotype."

"Surely one of the strangest experiences a person can have is suddenly to step out into the streets," wrote Griffin, "and find that the entire white society is convinced that an individual possesses qualities and characteristics which that person knows he does *not* possess." He was not referring to the fact that he appeared to be a Negro to whites when he was in disguise; rather, he was saying that anyone who is viewed as a stereotype rather than as an individual must feel this strangeness, regardless of how often it happens. "I am not speaking here only of myself," he pointed out. "This is the mind-twisting experience of every black person I know." But until Griffin had created his disguise, he had not realized how perplexing this sense of being perceived as a one-dimensional stereotype instead of as a multi-dimensional person could be. Of course, what is strangest of all, is that such stereotyping persists.

Authentic Experience

Ultimately, all questions about the authenticity of *Black Like Me*—like the questions about his motivations for attempting to become a Negro—cannot be "answered" in any definitive way; complex subjectivity cannot be distilled to a precise point of objectivity.

Yes, he was a white man in disguise, and, yes, beneath that appearance of blackness dwelled a privileged member of Southern society deeply conditioned by the mythology of race. But Griffin was not an ordinary Southern white male, or his crossing the line would have been in search of fantasy rather than truth. Yes, he was a "make-believe Negro," but what happened to him was not fiction. Most significantly, how he responded to what happened—to what was done to him and to those black people he encountered—awakened him and changed his life.

Yes, *Black Like Me* only approximates "the horror of the Negro's situation," and it is true that we "cannot put a white man in a Negro's place for, deep down, the white man understands that he is free," pointed out the reviewer in *Negro Digest*, "and the rules governing the Negro's life simply do not apply to him."

The University of Human Experience

Yes, Griffin could escape—and did. But could he have escaped the pursuit of the two bullies in New Orleans, or would it have been wise to push aside the bus driver's arm that kept the black passengers from the restroom facilities at the bus stop in Mississippi? Could he have escaped by saying, "Hey, time out now, I'm only playacting, I'm really white like you!" to that white driver of the bus?

While being chased by the bullies in New Orleans, was his terror "make-believe" or would it have been real only if he had been an actual black man? His fear was real because it was human fear. When he backed down from the threat of that bus driver, was he feeling fake fear and contrived humiliation or were his feelings exactly like those of the black passengers? Yes, he could escape *eventually*, but not by becoming white in an instant.

Stokely Carmichael, the civil-rights activist and early proponent of Black Power, once remarked that *Black Like Me* was "an excellent book—*for whites.*" Griffin could not have missed this comment, because it was printed in bold type (and in English) on the back cover of the Swedish edition of *Black Like Me*. But he never took issue with such comments during the 1960s and 1970s because he agreed with that assessment.

However, a generation later, during the mid-1980s, and certainly now [1997], thirty-five years after the book's original publication, that opinion is incorrect. It is wrong because today's readers of *Black Like Me*—most of whom are students in grades six through high school—have no direct knowledge of racism or segregation as it was experienced in the 1960s, regardless of their ethnicity. There has been voluminous testimony over the years—from students and educators both black and white—attesting to the fact that the book opened their minds to the evil of racism and evoked compassion in their hearts for fellow human beings.

Despite Its Stated Goal, *Black Like Me* Reinforces the Idea That Blacks and Whites Are Inherently Different

Kate Baldwin

Kate Baldwin teaches American Studies in the Weinberg College of Arts and Sciences at Northwestern University in Evanston, Illinois. Her research focuses on the intersection of race, ethnicity, and gender in twentieth-century American political thought.

In the following selection—excerpted from an article examining the anti-Communist overtones of Black Like Me—*Baldwin argues that by assuming that he must dye his skin in order to "pass" as African American, John Howard Griffin inadvertently demonstrates his own firm faith in the inherent and essential differences between blacks and whites. Furthermore, Baldwin argues that Griffin's tendency to seek out African American companionship in the poorest neighborhoods betrays his unexamined but powerful association between blacks and poverty.*

*B*lack Like Me first appeared in *Sepia* in 1960, serialized in three parts which were compiled in book form a year later. Marketed as a riveting racial exposé, *Black Like Me* was widely reviewed and quickly became a best-seller by claiming to have uncovered "what it is like, really like, to be a Negro in the deep South today." Thus, both the film and the written version of *Black Like Me* contend with the problematic of presenting anthropological "truths." Although they use different technologies to achieve this end, both mediums are concerned

Kate Baldwin, "Black Like Who? Cross-Testing the 'Read' Lines of John Howard Griffin's *Black Like Me*," *Cultural Critique 40*, Fall 1998. Copyright © 1998 by The University of Minnesota Press. All rights reserved. Reproduced by permission.

with presenting their story as "immediate" and "unmediated." The choices of genre reflect this concern, the film through a "documentary" style and the book through a first-person confessional. Without the presence of an audible narrative voice, the film must work to recuperate its hero as white so as to "speak" authoritatively in the same way ensured by the mode of written confessional. In both cases, *Black Like Me* recruits its modes of communication in order to produce the pathos of precisely the racial and sexual differentiation that it is the texts' slated purposes to deny. This is not to say that the texts are the same, but rather that both the hand of the writer and the hand of the director grapple with similar structural problematics for which they both, however coincidentally, come up with approximate solutions based on the demands of each of their respective genres.

Reinforcing White Authority

For example, at the same time that the author attempts to inscribe himself within a "black" persona, his narrative creates a disjunctive space where his "whiteness" always persists in framing his blackness. Because in both the film and the book our perception of Griffin's race is presumably based on a misreading in which the body proves to be an unreliable source for the revelation of his identity, the dissembling space of Griffin's passing produces a continual "error" of identity that the reader/viewer is always intended to register. Thus, although passing as a topic claims to question boundaries of difference, the narratives' apparatuses of "reading" not only underscore but in fact teach us about the necessary difference between white and black. The sympathetic reader/viewer was thus reassured that the rift in the color line forged by Griffin's actions—and emblematic of gains in black civil rights—remained superficial. Attempting to do away with race as a meaningful category through its claim that skin color makes no difference, this passing narrative repeatedly reminds us that skin color makes all the difference. . . .

Like the traditional slave narrative, Griffin's text turns to a white person to preface and testify first-hand to the authenticity of the tale to follow as written by a black person. In Griffin's text, however, both white authenticator and black authenticated are, of course, himself. As it has been suggested, the tradition of the "authentication" of African American narratives legitimates not only the text but also the author's personhood. In Griffin's text we encounter a modulation of this structure of authentication: the process of human legitimization undergirds a "good faith" liberal politics in which the "black" person possesses the ability to place on the well-meaning "white" person an "authentic" antiracist personhood through the very fact of association. . . .

A Kind of Minstrel Show

So can we trust the words of "experience" presented to us in this book? Griffin's claim to veracity relies on his own notions about blackness prior to his conversion. These enable him to privilege his own unfortunate case of blackness: he becomes both the "victim/black" and is simultaneously able to garner sympathy from whites precisely because he has at the same time become the "savior/white" of the southern black. But when Griffin "testifies" to his experiences in book form, he implicitly accepts the limits of testimony. These limits are imposed by the act of seeing, which, as Shoshana Felman has argued, once conjured by memory "to *address* another, to impress upon a listener, to *appeal* to a community" designs the narrative that will become his story. Conventional understandings of passing as subversive displace such limitations, which is to say that no thing exists outside of the boundaries Griffin himself constructs that could or would make him a "black" man. Likewise as readers and spectators, we ourselves are made to witness a failure to relate the "true" story as promised; and if Griffin's book bears false witness, then the uniqueness of Griffin's story is simply his unsuccessful attempt to "find out what it is really like to be a Negro in the deep South today." But what, you may ask, can a false passing mean if passing is itself premised on false assumptions of difference?

One way of shaping this question into a concrete historical framework would be to see, as Eric Lott [in his essay "White Like Me: Racial Cross-Dressing and the Construction of American Whiteness"] does, Griffin's traversal of racial boundaries as an enactment of "interracial" bonding, such as had been heretofore most prominently realized in the form of blackface minstrelsy. Unlike minstrelsy, however, in which white anxieties over racial difference were projected onto the stage so that a minstrel could either embody or act them out, Griffin's text serves as an appeal to racial solidarity that works with the idea of sameness in order to articulate difference. Unlike the white audience at a minstrel show, the reactions of whites *and* blacks enabled Griffin to assert that he was both white and black simultaneously, or an embodiment of the sameness of mankind. However, like the white audience at a minstrel show, Griffin was aware of the difference between himself as "white" and himself as "black," and it is this difference that his text articulates in the form of false witness to his own story. Whereas Griffin's text claims that he "passed," what his text reveals are the anxieties of an author who did not pass, who perhaps even sensed the inevitable failure of passing in a world where there are no reliable measures of racial difference. Griffin's reservations are masked in blackface so that, in the same way that when Griffin is black we presumably cannot "see" his whiteness, his story has become invisible.

An Unexamined Linking of Race and Class

That whiteness as a race affords itself invisibility is nowhere better evidenced than the moment at which Griffin claims, "The Griffin that was had become invisible." Thus assured of its constitutive transparency, whiteness can function as a measure of mankind and, in contradistinction, blackness becomes an essence through its ability to be discerned visually. This reality of blackness is an assertion that contradicts Griffin's presumption that skin color makes no difference. In fact, his whole project reasserts the necessity of racial difference as based singularly on skin shade—for how else does Griffin purport to become black but by darkening his skin? In stark contrast to Ralph Ellison's *Invisible Man* (in which the black man feels himself to be invisible), Griffin's task will be to come to terms with the face with which he feels "no companionship." This is his black face, the face that he believes makes him *visible*. But what the reader is supposed to see, of course, depends on a whole series of pseudo-transparencies.

For example, in both the book and the film, Griffin seeks out the poor area of town in order to find "Negroes." This undergirding of class-inflected racial categorization supports the entire premise of the story and in so doing serves to solidify racial difference as insurmountable inasmuch as black and white move in distinct social spheres. This is not only a lesson in racial difference, but a lesson in domestic policy. The rupture in the color line, we are taught, serves to bolster national solidarity: let poverty fall where it may. When Griffin asserts that the "black man is wholly a Negro, a second-class citizen," he uses race to reference caste. The implication is that it is wiser to let a "white man" tell the story of the Negroes, because by this fit-or-acquit kind of logic a "white man" is a "first-class" citizen, and therefore neither black nor a Negro. Put another way, because Griffin insists that once his face is darkened he "is" black, it follows that Griffin would be the exception to the rule that meshes blacks and Negroes. That is,

Griffin would be the only "black" man who was not a second-class citizen, which would mean, of course, that he was really "white"—according to the requirements of his own text. . . .

Race, Gender, and Powerful Taboos

A scene which illustrates the mechanisms of gender differentiation within the racializing process ensues. Griffin has secluded himself in his hotel room, desperate to contact his wife and family. In commencing to write a letter to his wife, he finds that his "conditioning as a Negro, and the immense sexual implications with which racists in my culture bombarded me, cut me off, even in my most intimate self, from any connection with my wife." The notion of communion between a black man and his white wife stimulates Griffin's anxiety about similitude. And yet the shape of blackness which emerges between Griffin and his wife is, as Lott contends, "a terrifying plenitude that must be sabotage." Griffin's fear turns to physiological difference to subtend the myth that all black men are overtly sexual. In so doing, Griffin superimposes his own conditioning not, as he would like to think, as a black man, but as a Southern gentleman whose "instincts" force him to "struggle against the estrangement." Although he would like to imagine that he had "intellectually liberated himself from the prejudices which our Southern culture inculcates in us, these prejudices were so profoundly indredged in me that at the emotional level I was in no way liberated" ("The Intrinsic Other"). Griffin cannot bear the thought of a black man contacting his white wife. Thus, despite his intentions to break the color barrier, Griffin finds himself—a white Southerner—policing that very line he presumably set out to sever.

Black Like Me Is About Humanity, Not Race

Sarfraz Manzoor

Sarfraz Manzoor is a British journalist and documentary film-maker, as well as a frequent contributor to the Guardian, *a major daily newspaper in the UK.*

Manzoor was born in Pakistan and moved to Great Britain with his family as a small child; in many regards, he notes, the experience of recent Indian and Pakistani immigrants to Great Britain roughly approximates that of modern African Americans. In the following article Manzoor reflects on the enduring popularity and importance of John Howard Griffin's Black Like Me, *which in 2011 marked the fiftieth anniversary of its first publication. Manzoor shares his own experience reading the book as a teen. While he acknowledges that, in many respects, this book has aged poorly—Griffin's prose seems more overwrought with each passing year, and the narrative itself seems increasingly unlikely—he points out that the book's lasting significance has less to do with the writing or the details of Griffin's experience than with the enduring problems of bigotry and discrimination that plague Western democracies.*

One day in 1964 John Howard Griffin, a 44-year-old Texan journalist and novelist, was standing by the side of the road in Mississippi with a flat tyre. He saw a group of men approaching him. Griffin assumed the men were heading over to assist him but instead they dragged him away from his car and proceeded to beat him violently with chains before leaving him for dead. It took Griffin five months to recover from the assault. The attack was not random; the beating represented a particularly brutal form of literary criticism: Griffin was being punished for having written a book. *Black Like Me*, the book in question, had been published three years earlier in November 1961 and it had led to its author being both venerated and vilified. Griffin, a lantern-jawed and chestnut-haired white man, deliberately darkened his skin and spent six weeks travelling through the harshly segregated southern states of America, revisiting cities he knew intimately, in the guise of a black man. On the opening page Griffin set out the question he was attempting to answer: "What is it like to experience discrimination based on skin colour, something over which one has no control?" No white man could, he reasoned, truly understand what it was like to be black, because black people would never tell the truth to outsiders. "The only way I could see to bridge the gap between us was to become a Negro," Griffin writes. "I decided I would do this."

The Shock of Unrecognition

He visits a dermatologist who prescribes medication usually given to victims of vitiligo (a disease that causes white spots to appear on the patient's skin) and he supplements the medication with sessions under a sun-lamp and by shaving his hair and rubbing a stain into his skin. In one of the most powerful passages in the book Griffin describes the shock of seeing his new self in the mirror for the first time. "In the flood of light against white tile, the face and shoulders of a stranger," he writes, "a fierce, bald, very dark Negro glared at me from the glass. He in no way resembled me . . . I had expected to see myself disguised, but this was something else. I was imprisoned in the flesh of an utter stranger, an unsympathetic one with whom I had no kinship . . . I looked into the mirror and saw reflected nothing of the white John Griffin's past. No, the reflections led back to Africa, back to the shanty and the ghetto, back to the fruitless struggles against the mark of blackness."

Startled by how little of himself he recognises, Griffin sets off on his journey and is further shocked by how little he recognises of his own country: the man who shines his shoes every day does not recognise him, the restaurants he usually eats in are no longer open to him, and he has to plan ahead if he wants to use the bathroom or drink from a water fountain. White folks either treat him with extravagant politeness— when they are on the hunt for black girls or they want to inquire about his sex life—or they give him what Griffin describes as "the hate stare". "Nothing can describe the withering horror of this," he writes, "you feel lost, sick at heart before such unmasked hatred, not so much because it threatens you as because it shows humans in such an inhuman light. You see a kind of insanity, something so obscene the very obscenity of it terrifies you. I felt like saying 'What in God's name are you doing to yourself?'" Being exposed to the hate stare, witnessing racism from the other side, leaves Griffin sad and angry; he grieves at how "my own people could give the hate stare, could shrivel men's souls, could deprive humans of rights they unhesitatingly accord their livestock". He concludes that "the Negro is treated not even as a second-class citizen but as a tenth-class one."

Griffin's Life Experience

Griffin's outrage at this injustice was rooted in his own life. He was studying in France at the outbreak of the second world war and joined the French resistance, helping to smuggle Jewish children to Britain. Having witnessed the consequences of racism against Jews he became more sensitive to the plight of black people in America. Griffin had been temporarily blinded during the war after being blasted with shrapnel. He recovered his sight two years before embarking on the journey

James Whitmore and Roscoe Lee Browne in the 1964 film adaptation of Black Like Me. © Everett Collection.

he described in *Black Like Me*, and the book can be read as a reaction to the lessons he learnt while sightless. "The blind," he would later write, "can only see the heart and intelligence of a man, and nothing in these things indicates in the slightest whether a man is white or black."

Black Like Me was Griffin's effort to persuade America to open its eyes. The first extracts from the book were published by *Sepia* magazine, and immediately he found himself the target of hostile attention. He received death threats, and an effigy of him was hung in Dallas, his home town, prompting Griffin and his family to go into exile in Mexico, where he did further work on the book. When it was published, he crisscrossed the country delivering lectures on his experiences; *Black Like Me* was translated into 14 languages, sold more than 10m copies, was adapted into a film and is still taught in schools and colleges across the US.

Encountering *Black Like Me* as a Teen

I was 16 years old and in college when I first read *Black Like Me*. I can vividly recall the impact it made on me: as an Asian teenager growing up in the 1980s I felt like a second-class citizen. There wasn't any literature that I had come across that spoke directly to my experience and so I embraced the literature of black America. I read the speeches of Martin Luther King, Richard Wright's *Native Son* and Ralph Ellison's *Invisible Man*, but *Black Like Me* struck an especially powerful chord partly because of Griffin's rage at the injustice of racism. In my own case, *Black Like Me* was not prophetic. Does it have any relevance 50 years after it was published?

Today the idea of a white man darkening his skin to speak on behalf of black people might appear patronising, offensive and even a little comical. Griffin felt that by blacking up he had "tampered with the mystery of existence", which sounded profound when I read it at 16, but now seems typical of Griffin's rather portentous prose, which occasionally makes one doubt the credibility of what he is describing. Would the doctor who administered the medication really have told him, on shaking his hand and waving him goodbye, "now you go into oblivion"? Later Griffin notes that when he sits down to write to his wife, he finds he is unable to do so: "The observing self," he recalled, "saw the Negro write 'Darling' to a white woman. The chains of my blackness would not allow me to go on." This, to me, lacks plausibility. Other questions emerge in the rereading: how is it that a 39-year-old white man can pass himself as black simply by darkening his skin and shaving his hair? Did no one notice his Caucasian features and become sceptical of the white man with weirdly dark skin? It is also striking how confidently Griffin seems able to inhabit the black mindset and speak for all black men, within, it seems, only days of starting his journey. Despite these misgivings, *Black Like Me* remains for me a brutal record of the indignities suffered by blacks in segregated America; it is also a reminder of how, in some respects, things have progressed.

Black Like Me and Barack Obama

Three months before its publication, Barack Obama was born in Hawaii. It is fascinating to speculate on Griffin's response had he been told, while on his odyssey through the segregated south, that a baby boy born to a Kenyan man would within 50 years be president of the United States. Obama's occupancy of the White House is, one could argue, emphatic proof that the world depicted in *Black Like Me* is history.

Obama's mother was white—but he made an explicit decision, which he describes in his memoir *Dreams From My Father*, to embrace a black identity. This self-conscious immersion into blackness led him to move to Chicago, to become active in the church, to familiarise himself with the canon of black literature and the civil rights movement so that he could claim his presidential hopes represented the fulfilment of the civil rights dream. Obama's case is of course different to Griffin's, but in one sense he, too, was not born black—he became black.

A Universal Story of Persecution

The similarities between Obama and Griffin are not, however, the primary reason why *Black Like Me* still speaks to us from a distance of 50 years; it resonates because its true topic is not race but humanity. Today in the US and elsewhere, Muslims have replaced blacks as the minority who are demonised, stereotyped and dehumanised. "To be a Muslim in America now is to endure slings and arrows against your faith," a recent cover story in *Time* magazine declared, "not just in the schoolyard and the office but also outside your place of worship and in the public square, where some of the country's most powerful mainstream religious and political leaders unthinkingly (or worse, deliberately) conflate Islam with terrorism and savagery."

Look at the footage of the protests against the inaccurately dubbed "Ground Zero Mosque" [in New York City]—the expressions on the faces of the protesters seem eerily familiar. The footage may be in colour, but it brings to mind grainy black and white archive film of protests against integration. The hate stare, described so starkly by Griffin, scarred the faces of these protesters. There is a man with a black father in the White House, but there is also another black man, Herman Cain, who is seeking the Republican nomination [in 2012] to become the next president, who has said that any Muslim serving in his administration would be forced to take a loyalty test.

"The Negro. The South. These are details," Griffin wrote in his preface. "The real story is the universal story—one of men who destroy the souls of other men. It is the story of the persecuted, the defrauded, the feared and detested." As long as one group persecutes, fears and detests another, *Black Like Me* will, sadly, remain essential reading.

Black Like Me Is Regaining Popularity Among African Americans in the Twenty-First Century

Jay Copp

Jay Copp is the senior editor for the headquarters edition of the Lions Clubs International publication LION Magazine *and a widely published writer.*

In the following article Copp explores the evolving reception of John Howard Griffin's Black Like Me *among African American readers and critics. Although the book was initially warmly received, many black writers and activists grew to resent the demand for a white-authored book on the degrading injustices suffered by African Americans when there were already many excellent accounts written by blacks and spanning many years and geographic areas. Throughout the 1960s and 1970s blacks' views of Griffin's work dimmed. Over the last couple of decades, however, the book has become more popular among blacks— especially educators—for its consistent ability to catalyze honest and open discussions of race among students of diverse backgrounds, something that has become increasingly challenging in the United States, even as race relations have steadily improved.*

Forty years have passed since the publication of *Black Like Me*, the searing account of a white Texan who dyed his skin black and encountered hatred and distrust among white Southerners. The book's Jim Crow era of lynchings and segregated lunch counters is long gone. But *Black Like Me* has endured.

The book's staying power is especially evinced by its new-found respect among African-Americans. First hailed and then scorned by some blacks, *Black Like Me* is finding favor again among blacks who are dismayed by a lack of progress in race relations.

A Vital Resource for Educators

"There is a real underground movement about the book. I get calls on it at least once a week," says Robert Bonazzi of Fort Worth, Texas, author of *Man in the Mirror: John Howard Griffin and the Story of 'Black Like Me.'* "It changed people's minds. It's still changing minds. It even makes a difference with young blacks, who don't have any knowledge of the segregation era."

The book has sold more than 10 million copies, but numbers alone don't measure its popularity or influence. *Black Like Me* has entered the canon of modern works educators treasure for their literary, historical, and humanistic value, along with *To Kill a Mockingbird, The Jungle, Animal Farm.* From grade school to college, curricula across America use the book as a springboard for discussion about racism, diversity, and multiculturalism.

Author John Howard Griffin was a deeply religious man, desperate to build a bridge between whites and blacks. His six-week odyssey through the South as a black person was a dark journey into racism. He was flashed the "hate stare" by dozens of white strangers, stalked by a young white man, barred by a white bus driver on a long trip from leaving the bus to use a restroom and insulted and disrespected by whites in nearly every encounter.

Uniquely Suited to Confront Racism

Griffin was uniquely qualified to confront racism. He was born in 1920 into a middle-class Dallas family. Studying in France at the outbreak of World War II, he provided medical treatment to ravaged black Senegalese soldiers used as cannon fodder against the Nazis by the French. He joined the French resistance and bravely spirited Jewish refugees out of the country.

Later, as a US soldier, he lived like a native among tribesmen in a remote Pacific island, where his skills counted for little in the harsh jungle. Blinded by an enemy shell, he spent a decade without vision, encountering the prejudices and stereotypes of the seeing world. Griffin miraculously recovered his sight in 1957.

"Being blind was a great experience," he told *The Washington Post*. "As a Southerner all the stereotypes I'd been brought up with, the speech patterns that blacks were supposed to have, the appearance, all those delusions had to go out the door."

African Americans Embrace the Book

Blacks warmly embraced *Black Like Me* in 1961. Journalist Louis Lomax praised the book in the *Saturday Review*: "There is a saying among Negroes that no white man, no matter how hard he tries, can really understand what it's like to be black in America. John Howard Griffin has come closer to this understanding than any white man that I know." *Ebony* magazine did a lavish photo spread in 1964 on a movie based on the book. Griffin became a welcomed fixture in the Civil Rights movement, strategizing with Martin Luther King Jr., Dick Gregory, and other black leaders.

Yet the book also stirred resentment as black consciousness rose. Black nationalist Stokely Carmichael dismissed it as "an excellent book for whites." Writer Shelby Steele said he disliked the book when he read it in the 1960s because it reduced the richness of black experience to being victims of white prejudice.

William Spriggs of the National Urban League in Washington was a teenager in the 1970s. The book first struck him as both patronizing and passé. "There was this window of opportunity in the '70s. People were willing then to engage in a cordial debate about race," he says.

Regressive Race Relations

"Today there's been a regression [in race relations]," says Mr. Spriggs, the director of the Urban League's Institute for Opportunity and Equality. "The book is relevant to our times. We're no longer in the Jim Crow era, but blacks are still followed. It's still hard to get a taxi. We're still denied jobs because of race."

Whites did not hide their contempt for Griffin as a black person. That has not changed as much as people might assume, says Sandra Jackson, an associate professor of education and director of the Center for Culture and History of the Black Diaspora at DePaul University in Chicago. "Some of the experience [of racism] is still in your face. Look at the black man [James Byrd Jr.] who was dragged from a truck in Texas [in 1998]. That was out in the open," she says. Blacks are nevertheless cautious about giving too much credence to a book by a white on the black experience. "Griffin could return to what he used to be," says Ms. Jackson. "It's like a man trying to be a woman for a day. Most men live for 78 years. That's just one day."

More authentic accounts of the black experience are found in works by Richard Wright, James Baldwin, and other great black writers. "Griffin proved a point about the absurdity of treatment based on skin color, but it's ridiculous to suppose that African-American culture exists entirely in response to white racism," says Lawrence Jackson, an assistant professor of English at Howard University in Washington.

Sparking Honest Conversations

Black Like Me is required reading in schools nationwide. Prof. Peter Morgan of the University of West Georgia in Carrollton uses it in a class on Young Adult Literature for aspiring teachers. "Literature helps students—and student teachers—develop empathy, to see the world from multiple perspectives," he says. "*Black Like Me* is especially potent in this respect. Students who are somewhat jaded by TV movies and preachy novels are stunned by the new insights they get into the real world of their parents and grandparents."

Black Like Me was initially praised for its journalistic snapshot image of the South. It is now praised for transcending its time and place in exploring universal themes of identity and race. "The book is useful as a metaphor about walking in someone else's shoes," says Jackson of DePaul. "It takes people out of their comfort zone and gives them insights they might not have had."

After Griffin's account was published (initially as a series in the black magazine *Sepia*), he was hung in effigy in Mansfield, where he lived. Death threats forced him to move his family to Mexico. Later in life, he became disillusioned with the lack of progress in race relations. His final project was official biographer of monk Thomas Merton. He never finished, dying in 1980. Left unfinished too, in his own mind, was the improvement in race relations he wanted his book to effect.

Teachers tell another story. Morgan says the book continues to arouse debate and insight. "There are always students who say, 'But it's not like that anymore,'" says Morgan. "But then another student will say, 'Well . . . ,' and the class begins to share anecdotes that demonstrate that old ideas run close to the surface for many."

Analyzing the Enduring Effectiveness of *Black Like Me*

Hugh Rank

Hugh Rank is most noted for his analysis of argumentation and persuasive styles in a variety of media. His books on such rhetoric include Language and Public Policy, The Pitch: How to Analyze Advertising, *and* The Pep Talk: How to Analyze Political Language.

This essay is notable in that it was written just a few years after the initial publication of Black Like Me *and represents a contemporaneous reaction to the book, relatively free from the influence of the book's later reputation. Rank explores the complexity of what otherwise seems to be a straightforward—even somewhat ill-organized—memoir. Rank especially notes the subtlety of the book's structure, through which John Howard Griffin presents himself as both a "regular Joe" struggling to understand an overwhelming situation and as a sort of undercover agent. These two identities are especially powerful in persuading readers to identify with Griffin on a personal level, and thus they are integral to* Black Like Me*'s ongoing effectiveness.*

In 1959, John Howard Griffin, a white Southern novelist, disguised himself as a Negro and traveled through the South to experience "what it is like to be a Negro in a land where we keep the Negro down." The brief narrative account of this experience is recorded in *Black Like Me,* a book which won the *Saturday Review*'s Anisfield-Wolf award in 1962 for its contribution toward race relations.

Today, almost ten years after Griffin's unique tour, this book continues to have wide sales both in a popular market

Hugh Rank, "The Rhetorical Effectiveness of *Black Like Me,*" *The English Journal,* September 1968.

and in classroom adoptions. By January 1968, *Black Like Me* was in its thirty-first paperback printing, a printing history which the publisher described (in a letter to me) as "quite unusual . . . and still going strong." The book appears deceptively simple and can be read merely as a piece of popular journalism on a timely subject. But, in a market now glutted with writings about racial problems, any single book which manages to have such a continued attraction for a large portion of the available audience deserves further attention to determine the basis for its popularity. In brief, why is *Black Like Me* rhetorically effective?

Rhetoric must be considered here, not in the limited terms of organization and style, but in the wider, more classical, sense which is concerned also with the *ethos* of the writer and the relationship between the writer and the audience. Too often readers have ignored the Aristotelian insistence on the variety of rhetorical appeals available to the writer. As a consequence, they have been unable to analyze the quality of a work which doesn't fit into a more restricted approach to rhetoric.

The Significance of Structure

Black Like Me, for example, could be found deficient if judged solely on terms of organization and style. Using such criteria, some may call the book "a rough piece of hack work" or "a rush job." Even the author himself, in the preface, apologizes for its "crudity and rawness," an ambiguous remark which can be read in relation to either content or form. Yet even here, on its weakest points, a defense can be made that the book has a better structure than most readers note. This is not to claim that *Black Like Me* is a masterpiece; it is a rough-hewn book, hammered and forged, unlike Griffin's smoothly tooled novels. However, the structural and thematic elements found in the work are often overlooked or are overshadowed by the "message" of the book. But Griffin is not unaware of structure because his background in musicology has seriously influenced his strategy of writing. Griffin's best novel, *The Devil Rides Outside*, for instance, takes its structure from one of Beethoven's Final Quartets, and his current [never-finished] novel-in-progress, *Passacaglia*, is structured on this complex musical form.

Black Like Me is seemingly haphazard in its structure, simply a random series of journal entries in his diary. Nevertheless, any journal is a *selection* of incidents and experiences; even the most unconsciously written report would tend to stress certain things held by the writer to be of greater value than the other, non-reported, daily experiences. Structurally, the book is divided into three main parts: a brief "prelude" introduces his plan to disguise himself, the main body of the book concerns his actual tour as a black man, and an extended "epilogue" describes some of the consequences of his experiment.

The most noticeable point here is that the "epilogue" violates the standard narrative pattern because it takes up almost one-fifth of the book. What happens is that *Black Like Me* changes to *White Liberal Like Me* as Griffin records another aspect of racism—how it is to be a white liberal crusader in the South. The later *consequences* of violating the existing social mores are given more emphasis by this seemingly undue proportion of space given to the "epilogue." Within this last section the sense of a *continuing* harassment is given by the writer's wider spacing of dates for journal entries. His experience as a black man lasts only three weeks (in November); his experience as a "marked man" extends for nine more months in the book. If Griffin were to write a postscript today [in 1968] to *Black Like Me*, he could continue relating nine more *years* of harassment by racists and hate groups who have continued their attacks upon him. Thus, the length of the "epi-

A scene from the 1964 film adaptation of Black Like Me. © AF Archive/Alamy.

logue," which seems at first to be too long in proportion to the book, actually serves to underline a very important part of Griffin's experience.

Repetition and Juxtaposition

The forward motion of the narrative is sustained by two major suspense devices. In the early parts of the book, the reader's anticipation is aroused as to whether or not Griffin's disguise will be discovered by either black or white, friend or foe. In the last section of the book, the ominous threats of violence are increased. The book ends the day after the threatened lynch mob fails to appear, an apt time to make a quick ending to avoid a lengthy anti-climax to the secondary theme. Within these two major devices which propel the story forward, there is also a subtle under-current of motion which prevents the book from becoming static. Griffin is always in motion— either walking on the streets or hitchhiking or riding on the busses—and even when he rests temporarily in a hotel room or on a farm the sense of motion is given by his preparations to go on the road again.

Other structural devices which deserve attention are Griffin's frequent use of repetition and juxtaposition. Key themes are repeated in the book showing an apparently unconscious selection of critical issues. While the reaction of Griffin to the word "ni-----" gets only one paragraph, in spite of the word's omnipresence, the bus episodes get a great deal of repeated attention, probably because of the important symbolic nature of the bus integration attempts going on at the time under Martin Luther King's leadership. There is also a major repetition of focus on sexuality and the fantastic stereotypes and myths of Negro sexuality, an area, according to many scholars, of critical psychological problems between black and white in the South. But Griffin's major repetition seems to be the idea that he is the "same man," whether his skin is white or black. The "same man" theme recurs throughout the book, the dominant plea for brotherhood and tolerance.

Juxtaposition of contrasting incidents or contrasting characters to heighten the irony is commonly used. In some of the most intense sections, two divergent things will play counterpoint to each other. For instance, in both "sexuality" sections, the perversity emphasized in the beginning of the section is countered by a discussion of [philosopher Jacques] Maritain's ideas on, *caritas* [a selfless, compassionate love] and by a description of the poor Negro family in the swamps, a living example of such genuine love. In the closing pages of the book, both Griffin's hopes for progress in race relations (as seen in the analysis of Atlanta) and his fears of a violent black reaction are linked together. This ambivalence of his feeling here is certainly understandable in view of the changing moods of race relations in the past few years [of the late 1960s], but Griffin's attitude is noteworthy as it was written at a time when many people involved in the civil rights movement were more optimistic about progress.

"Black-and-White" Juxtapositions

Such frequent use of juxtaposition has encouraged some criticism that the book is too "black and white." The good guys are black; the bad guys, white. Such a reaction is understandable because the book does involve emotional response on an issue which many readers are affected by a pre-conditioning. But if the choice of "characters," or persons described, is analyzed more closely, then the "black and white" criticism has less validity because Griffin attempts to show a whole spectrum of shades. While it is true that the bigotry of the white racist is emphasized, the reader is also introduced to a variety of other white men—a crusading liberal editor in the South, a Southern boy agonized by his own confusion about the problem, an obsequious Northern white "liberal," and, of course, the author himself. While there seem to be too many God-fearing, Bible-reading, kindly Negroes in parts of the book, the reader is also aware of the frustrated madman Christophe on the bus, the petty tyranny of the Negro shoeshine attendant to the beggar, the crudities of life in the back of the bus and in the ghetto, and all shades of black from Uncle Tom to black racist. Certainly a selection from the actual number of people encountered during the experience has been made to illustrate the many different types of people and their responses to the problem.

Although a defense of the structural and stylistic methods of Griffin can be extended, the reasons for the continued popularity and readability of *Black Like Me* are not primarily concerned with his organization and style. Nor are they simply the result of the widespread interest in all phases of the Negro problem, because this would not explain why this one book has had such a unique impact. What best explains the durability of *Black Like Me* can probably be described by the writer-reader relationship and the *ethos* of the writer.

Griffin as Undercover Agent

Personal narratives of Negroes frequently have created a close *sympathetic* reaction from the audience, but still, in our society, the gap between black and white exists. *Empathy*, the close identification of reader and writer in this case, is much easier to establish with a white narrator speaking to a predominantly white audience. *Black Like Me* has severe limitations because it has been written by a white man, but this book also gains a great deal because of the white narrator who has less of a gap to bridge between himself and his audience. For part of this white audience, the book may also be more credible and less likely to be accused of exaggeration, special pleading, or self-pity.

Another factor which helps to bring a closer empathy between reader and writer is Griffin's adoption of the "undercover agent" role, the solitary individual secretly in combat with an evil system. The popularity of this theme grows increasingly more widespread in twentieth-century literature as the actual presence of large organizations, massive institutions, and super-states becomes more obvious. Both the pulp writer and the literary craftsman have recently [since World War II] produced a wealth of stories concerning one man covertly fighting against the oppression of an unjust system. Griffin's adventure in *Black Like Me* parallels that of the spy, the prisoner-of-war [POW], or the "innocent prisoner" plotting alone, in secret, against the evil institution. Whether we consider the weekly TV episodes of POW escapes from Nazi camps or [Bernard] Malamud's prize-winning novel, *The Fixer*, we can see the powerful appeal being made to get the reader's empathy toward the individual who is at odds with an oppressive system. The satisfaction of this vicarious experience is apt to be widespread in a society concerned with the diminishing role of the individual.

The vicarious participation of the reader of *Black Like Me* is aided by the narrator's humility and self-effacement. Griffin establishes a favorable *ethos*, or image, by focusing on his work, on his experiment, rather than on any self-centered claims of heroism or daring for his unique adventure. In fact, by revealing his own fears and loneliness, he emphasizes his normality and makes it easy for the average reader to re-live his experience. Griffin's only personal claim is that he has tried to be objective: "I tried to see the whites' side, as I have all along. I have studied objectively the anthropological arguments, the accepted clichés about cultural and ethnic differences. . . . I have held no brief for the Negro. I have looked diligently for all aspects of 'inferiority' among them and I cannot find them. . . . When all the talk, all the propaganda has been cut away, the criterion is nothing but the color of skin. My experience proved that. They judged me by no other quality. My skin was dark."

Griffin as "Regular Guy"

Another aspect of the techniques used by Griffin to create a favorable *ethos* is his use of the "plain folks" approach. Griffin is just a "regular guy" trying to understand the situation. In reality, Griffin is much more than a "regular guy," a common man, or "plain folk." Whether one would emphasize his work in the French underground during the Second World War, his demonstrated musical ability as a pianist and musicologist (on Chopin), his philosophical research and writings (tutored by Jacques Maritain), or his ten-year period of blindness during which he wrote *The Devil Rides Outside* (a novel highly praised in Maxwell Geismar's *American Moderns*), the general conclusion would be that Griffin possesses not only a superior intellect but also is a man of rare courage, endurance, and integrity. Yet none of these accomplishments is mentioned in *Black Like Me*. If one were to consider the effect of such information added to the book, either in the text or in an introduction, it would seem that such biographical data would serve to elevate the status of the author, to emphasize the superiority of the author to the average reader. What would normally be a desirable thing to do, here would work against the empathy or close identification with the author which is so effective in *Black Like Me*.

The *ethos* of the writer communicated in this book is that of the "good man" searching for truth through a painful experiment. The informed reader will also be aware, from Griffin's occasional religious and literary allusions, that the image suggested can be described in terms of the Christian Humanist or Personalist, deeply concerned with bearing witness to his beliefs.

The mere fact that a "good man" writes a book does not automatically make the work good; enough poorly written tracts have been published by sincere people to prove that integrity alone is no substitute for craftsmanship. Yet Aristotle points out that the ethical appeal, the projection of the image of being a "good man," is often more effective than the logical or emotional appeals. Ideally, all three should function together for the most persuasive writing. In *Black Like Me*, the emotional appeal is obvious throughout the book; the logical appeal resides primarily in the concealed syllogism behind the "same man" theme. But the major strength of the book seems to be in the ethical appeal, in the ability both to convey the image of the "good man" and to achieve a close reader-writer empathy through the "plain folks" and "undercover agent" devices used naturally and unconsciously by the author in this situation.

Such reader empathy probably inspired the following anonymous tribute:

Open Letter to the White Nigger—John Howard Griffin

There are those, John, who could

Never listen to a black voice

Because it smelled so odd.

And so, you lived a lie

And wrote the truth.

Then somewhere, many where,

We read. And instead

Of fury, we felt grief.

For an hour, we were you

And you were black

And we were black like you.

Black Like Me Was Cold War Propaganda

Nelson Hathcock

Nelson Hathcock is an English professor at Saint Xavier University in Chicago.

In the following essay Hathcock argues that Black Like Me *is an important piece of pro-American Cold War propaganda. He points out that John Howard Griffin implicitly treats the South as the sole source of racial strife within the United States and an "un-American" region that is running contrary to national policy. This approach allowed Griffin to imply that America was battling, rather than enabling, the embarrassing domestic human rights violations for which it was then notorious. According to Hathcock,* Black Like Me *is the perfect piece of pro-American, anti-Communist propaganda because on the surface Griffin's tale appears to expose American hypocrisy, while the subtext argues that the most efficient—and just—path to racial harmony was free-market capitalist opportunity.*

The timing of *Black Like Me* was critical. It appeared at a propitious historical moment and ultimately aided in defining that moment. The Red Scare of the early fifties generated an outpouring of testimony, confession, and exposés by former Communists, which contributed to altering social attitudes toward the act of informing, and, I will argue briefly, anticipated [John Howard] Griffin as a racial "double-agent." A more important link between these texts and Griffin's is their narrative of disillusionment and revision, a process that Cold War liberals underwent on their way to ideological "higher ground."

Nelson Hathcock, "'A Spy in the Enemy's Country': *Black Like Me* as Cold War Narrative," *American Studies*, vol. 44, no. 3, Fall 2003. Copyright © American Studies. All rights reserved. Reproduced by permission.

Certainly, the broader historical backdrop to the book's success was America's emergence as one of two superpowers on the international stage. As Thomas Borstelmann observes, "Competing with the Soviet Union in the post-war world meant, by definition, maximizing the amount that other peoples saw of American life." The second-class status of African Americans focused attention upon the Jim Crow South. This development particularly conflicted with America's asserted role as "leader of the Free World," especially to countries breaking the shackles of colonialism. The so-called Third World became the audience for that drama of bipolar competition, and the non-white racial makeup of that audience challenged the United States severely. While legal segregation remained in place, American anti-colonial rhetoric rang false. In this atmosphere, the United States Information Agency (USIA) and the Voice of America (VOA) labored to gain acceptance abroad of the United States and its institutions. The U.S. policy of containment became a broadly disseminated trope [metaphor] of control for dealing with the radical, the transgressive, and the subversive *within* the society. This essay will show how *Black Like Me* promulgated a version of that trope, depicting the Deep South as a site of un-American "Otherness" in order to isolate and diminish its negative ramifications for the U.S. image abroad. However, representing the South as something to be controlled placed Griffin's text in a curious relation to the same federal government for which it was, in effect, performing a cultural mission. . . .

Cold War Paranoia

The paranoia of the early 1950s laid an important foundation for Griffin's exercise in domestic surveillance. Once America's nuclear monopoly had been broken in 1949, the idea of overt conflict with Russia became a grim nightmare. The Korean stalemate underscored the very real limitations of a "limited conflict." Domestic subversion became the antagonist of

Men drinking from segregated water fountains in the American South, circa 1960. View-point author Nelson Hathcock argues that Black Like Me *is pro-America Cold War propaganda that portrays the racist South as un-American.* © Bettmann/Corbis.

choice, while the efforts to root it out constituted an index of frustration, as [political researcher] Stephen Whitfield has suggested. From many quarters the theme sounded that American government, industry, education, and entertainment were rotten with a Communist element, and the only way to resist the "enemy within" was to adopt his tactics of disguise and subterfuge. The figure of the spy, first imaged as menace, was quickly transformed into hero, a process that would culminate in the glamorous apotheosis of James Bond in the 1960s. But that figure was preceded by the informer.

The work of the House Committee on Un-American Activities [HUAC], the Federal Bureau of Investigation, and other investigative bodies precipitated an outpouring of confessions and exposés by ex-Communists as the cultural prohibition against informing was revised. Americans had long held "rats," "finks," and "stool pigeons" in low regard, with the injunction against "tattling" being culturally reinforced from kindergarten. Now, however, the parade of "friendly witnesses," "informants," and "recovered patriots" who trooped before one agency after another made informing respectable. This shift of rhetoric and reconstructed esteem sprang from what [author of *Naming Names*, the definitive book on anti-Communist blacklisting in Hollywood] Victor Navasky has called "The Informer Principle," which "held not merely that there was nothing wrong with naming names, but that it was the litmus test, the ultimate evidence, the guarantor of patriotism." He points out as well that "the vulgar popular culture of the day . . . was openly dedicated to refurbishing the image of the anti-Communist informer." Griffin's testimony as a racial double-agent fits neatly into the slot prepared by the popular culture of the day—feature films, television and radio, and mass-market memoirs—that created a paradigm of the informant narrative and viewed reformers as patriotic, realistic, and tough. . . .

Reforming America's Image Overseas

Black Like Me not only adopts the superficial traits of the informant story—disguise, life among an enemy, transmission of information, and so on; it also dramatizes the liberal's journey from innocence to experience. In this recounting he presumes to speak both to an America afflicted with the liberal's dangerous moral myopia and to a world that sees what America does not. A series of statements in Griffin's first entry of the book (dated October 26, 1959) speaks to the question of the Cold War liberals' attempt to elevate the power of the subjective:

> If a white man became a Negro in the Deep South, what adjustments would he have to make? What is it like to experience discrimination based on skin color, something over which one has no control? . . .

> How else except by becoming a Negro could a white man hope to learn the truth?

This passage is important primarily because Griffin designates the problem site as the "Deep South," where Negroes experience discrimination and where "a white man" can learn about the "adjustments" to be made. That Griffin could just as "easily" have passed in, say, Pennsylvania and encountered similar treatment was seized upon a few years later by Southerner Walker Percy in his novel *The Last Gentleman* (1966), with its scathing caricature of Griffin as Forney Aiken, the "pseudo-Negro." And [civil rights activist] Malcolm X had insisted on numerous occasions that "Mississippi is anywhere south of the Canadian border." However, Griffin's assertion that the geographic South is the location of America's racial conflict becomes more vital later. The apparent powerlessness inherent in skin color is denied a few lines later by Griffin's literal and rhetorical proposition that he "becom[e] a Negro." Griffin's representation of his skin having no color becomes a canvas on which he can create the illusion of a racial identity. Contemporary scholars of "whiteness," such as Gayle Wald and Eric Lott, are troubled by Griffin's assumptions of entitlement to "the cultural knowledge of others." But the act of passing as an avenue to "the truth" is also congruent with the then-current liberal notion that subjective experience constitutes reality. . . .

Just as HUAC's witnesses might jar American complacency by attesting first-hand to the reality of an internal Communist threat (grossly overstated to further the domestic political containment), Griffin could, as Wald points out, "authenticate the existence of racism and thereby promote a level of white cross-racial understanding that he believed to be unavailable through more conventional modes of inquiry." The problem with this equation is that to many, particularly Southerners, Griffin himself became a part of a threat. From the heyday of the Communist Party USA in the 1920s and 1930s, the link between the party and issues of lynching, discrimination, and civil rights for African Americans had been overt. In the post-war world, that connection proved a serious liability for black activists because it furnished racist Southern white politicians and businessmen with the material for smear campaigns. Griffin's brand of liberalism came dangerously close to the same idealism from which Cold War liberals sought to distance themselves. . . .

Capitalism and Liberalism

Griffin's eventual stint in the showcase of the "New South"—Atlanta—provides his text with the element of hope that the containment narrative requires, but upon his arrival there, his outlook matches that of the weary, oppressed African Americans he has lived among: "I had arrived in Atlanta feeling that the situation for the Negro in the South was utterly hopeless—due to the racists' powerful hold on the purse strings of whites and Negroes alike; and due to the lack of unanimity among Negroes." For all Griffin's experience of reflexive hatred and simmering violence, he has concluded that the core of the problem is economic. Just as the USIA had planned to counter international communism by extolling the virtues of capitalism, Griffin's journey ends where promise abounds through economic reform. By the time he rides into Atlanta, Griffin could confess to considerable accord with [historian Arthur M.] Schlesinger's liberalism: "The modern American capitalist . . . has come to share many values with the American liberal: beliefs in personal integrity, political freedom and equality of opportunity." Economic opportunity began to function as propagandistic shorthand for democratic reform; in the South it was the antidote to racial oppression, and in the Third World, it was meant to defuse the revolutionary violence of Communist insurgency.

Like Schlesinger and the post-war liberals before him, Griffin recognizes the absolute necessity of an economy that provides equality of opportunity and reward, even if the structures of political power lag behind. A few years later (1964) [historian] Howard Zinn would document his own sojourn in the "enemy's country" with a surprisingly optimistic take on the longevity of segregation. He was convinced that white Southerners would gladly repudiate Jim Crow whenever economic pressure was brought to bear. Griffin's experience of Atlanta, however, is told from the perspective of his adopted racial status and substantiates the propagandistic aims of the text. Not for Griffin the black militants who were already beginning to wrestle with King and others for control of African American loyalties. *His* militants are capitalists—the heroes of an Atlanta reconstructed in the Washingtonian ideal of economic emancipation.

Capitalism as Cure

Griffin cites the arrival in Atlanta in the 1930s of two economists, L.D. Milton and J.B. Blayton, who began to put into action their ideas about black self-sufficiency. These men recognized that the black community's dependence upon white-owned banks and other financial sources would simply perpetuate its second-class status. Milton and Blayton preached the doctrine of financial consolidation, and their efforts resulted in the establishment of two banks from which the economic base of black Atlanta arose. Housing, education, and entrepreneurship all improved with the availability of loans, and the average black businessman gained leverage with white money-men. Standards of living crept higher, with, as Zinn would argue at almost the same time, the profit motive proving stronger than the will to segregate.

This narrative of capitalism as weapon against racial oppression seems just the kind of parable that the USIA would disseminate among the developing nations on the move. *Black Like Me* enacts a perfect snare—an international audience relishes what it thinks is one more exposure of American hypocrisy and African American oppression, only to be shown that the United States has the most effective remedy: the capitalist system. Griffin goes on to quote T.M. Alexander, one of the founders of the Southeastern Fidelity Fire Insurance Company, and Alexander's words have a curious ring: "There is no 'big Me' and 'little you.' We must pool all of our resources, material and mental, to gain the respect that will enable all of us to walk the streets with the dignity of American citizens." Black Atlanta's capitalism operates as a communal force; the mass behind the system gives it its power. No better description could be applied to that USIA catch-phrase "People's Capitalism." Implicit is the idea that the isolated mill worker in Alabama will eventually be absorbed into such a protective, empowering mass. However, for all his apotheosizing of capitalism, Griffin points out as well that Atlanta had all the democratic essentials in place: a populace united behind leaders of "high education, long vision and great dynamism"; an enlightened city administration; and a newspaper (the *Atlanta Constitution*) oriented in the tradition of Southern liberalism. No need for either riots or boycotts here.

Families Switch
Ethnic Identities

Lynn Elber

Lynn Elber is a television writer for AP Online.

In the following viewpoint, Elber discusses a television series in which families switch races, enacting the same experiment as John Howard Griffin's years later. The executive producer of Black.White. admits he did not realize how difficult it would be for whites and blacks to see the world through each other's eyes. Outside of the families' houses, racial attitude is expressed subtly by the public.

When writer John Howard Griffin turned his skin from white to dark and traveled the South in 1959 for a first-hand look at the depths of racism, he relied on a simple medical treatment and his wits.

Undercover Race Detectives

In the 21st century, such a journey requires Hollywood makeup wizardry, the well-honed conventions of both reality TV and documentary filmmaking, and two families, one black, one white, acting as undercover race detectives in Southern California.

As superficially different as FX's "Black.White." and Griffin's landmark book "Black Like Me" appear to be, they are brothers under the skin.

"Black.White." proceeds with open-minded seriousness as it leads viewers to a conclusion both obvious and powerful: race counts, for better and worse. Expressions of racism and racial identity change, but that bedrock truth remains.

Lynn Elber, "Families Swap Races on FX Reality Series," AP Online, February 16, 2006. Reproduced by permission.

Seeing the World Through Each Other's Eyes

"I didn't realize, more than anything, how hard it was going to be for whites and blacks to see the world through each other's eyes," said executive producer R.J. Cutler. "I didn't realize how genuinely different an experience it is to be a white American and a black American."

Cutler insisted the six-episode show, which begins March 8 on FX, doesn't "aspire in any way to say definitive things about race." But the participants and their actions do.

In a Los Angeles-area house, "Black.White." brings together Bruno Marcotulli, 47, his wife, Carmen Wurgel, 48, and her daughter Rose Bloomfield, 18, a white family from Santa Monica, and Brian Sparks, 41, wife Renee, 38, and their son, Nick, 17, a black Atlanta family.

Through artful makeup they swap races, if not perspectives.

"You see what you want to see," Marcotulli says at one point to Brian Sparks, dismissing Sparks' experiences with prejudice.

"And you don't see what you don't want to see," a frustrated Sparks replies.

Cutler, whose documentary films and TV series include the acclaimed "The War Room" and "American High," was joined by Ice Cube, the rapper, actor and producer, on the project proposed by FX Networks President John Landgraf.

"Don't believe the hype, everything in the world ain't black and white. Everybody ain't a stereotype. Just because I look wrong I'm about to do right," Cube sings in the title song, which also includes his sharp rejection of an oft-cited phrase: "Did you get your race card? Yo, what the hell is a race card?"

His hope for the project was to "expose the subtleties of racism, the layers of racism," the musician told The Associated Press. "Everybody thinks of a Klan man standing with a shotgun, yelling, 'Keep it white.'

"Everybody is worried about the guy with the black power, leather jacket on, Afro ... worried about those kind of people and not really knowing that racism is not just the obvious," Cube said.

The series' timing is notable, with race brought into renewed focus by Katrina and the disproportionate suffering it caused for blacks in New Orleans. But "Black.White." was conceived before the hurricane, Landgraf said.

He brought the idea of having two families trade races to Cutler, stressing that he wasn't looking for cheap conflict.

Not About Cheap Conflict

"I said, 'This is not cheesy, this is not about putting a white bigot ... in with black people and watching them beat the crap out of each other and watching sparks fly,'" Landgraf recalled. "And it certainly wasn't about some kind of makeup-driven freak show."

The families in "Black.White." are middle-class, the adults all college-educated. They received a modest fee for their participation, an FX spokesman said.

With special-effects makeup by Keith Vanderlaan and Brian Sipe that artfully used wigs, airbrushed skin paint and other elements, the families were transformed to a new ethnicity that could pass muster in varied settings.

Teenager Rose joined a poetry group with young blacks; Brian Sparks became a bartender at a place drawing white customers. The families also, in the best tradition of reality TV, shared a house in 2005 for the six weeks of production.

Cutler "wanted the families to live together, because a lot of discussion would be generated in each family coaching the other family on what it is to be white or to be black, and to pass or behave or act as white or black," Landgraf said.

Wurgel makes what she considers a black fashion statement, buying a dashiki for church, while Renee Sparks looks askance.

Confrontation

The housemates have revealing, sometimes heated clashes over their attitudes on race and the use of volatile epithets. One confrontation pits the black father, adamantly opposed to the "n-word," against his unconcerned teenage son.

For his part, Marcotulli consistently clings to his belief that any individual can erase bias by dint of sheer will and optimism.

Outside the house, attitudes are mostly, but not always, subtly expressed. In black makeup, Rose gets the brushoff when she applies for work at stores in a white area. One shopkeeper glances in a drawer and unconvincingly announces she's out of job applications.

Sitting in as a white woman on a focus group discussion on race, Renee Sparks is shocked to hear a young college student relate how he was cautioned to wash off the handshake of a black person.

"I thought, here it is, 2005, and people are still teaching their kids this," Sparks said in a recent interview with reporters.

Larry E. Davis, director of the University of Pittsburgh's Center on Race and Social Problems, lauds the series' concept. "Black Like Me" was a powerful work in its day; projects like "Black.White." have potential value for now, he said.

"It will bring (issues of race) into a context and a time frame and a reality that a new generation can comprehend, can relate to and understand," Davis said. The goal is to "keep hammering away, hammering way, hammering away at the problem."

Students' Accounts of Discrimination Enhance Their Understanding of *Black Like Me*

Jennifer Haberling and Brian White

Jennifer Haberling is a teacher in Hudsonville, Michigan, and was Michigan Teacher of the Year for 2008–2009. Brian White is a professor of English at Grand Valley State University in Allendale, Michigan.

Haberling taught Black Like Me *in an almost all-white high school in rural Michigan. Although Haberling—like many teachers—maintains that* Black Like Me *continues to be a very relevant text for twenty-first-century high-school students, she found that students in homogeneous communities were very resistant to seeing John Howard Griffin's account as more than simply a historical record. Inviting her students to compose fictional case studies of modern instances of discrimination set in their own community, Haberling found that many students actually offered thinly disguised records of actual instances of victimization. By actively engaging Griffin's text with their own experience, students overcame their own tendency to see racism as "over" and a thing of the past.*

In *Black Like Me*, John Howard Griffin, a White man, tells the story of his attempt to understand the lives and experiences of African Americans in the late 1950s and early 1960s by having his skin chemically darkened and living as a Black man. Griffin's account of the oppression, danger, and prejudice he experienced while disguised as an African American helped to open the eyes of the nation to the plight of people of color in the United States. Nearly fifty years after its initial publication, *Black Like Me* remains an important book, especially because so many in our society seem to be convinced that the struggle for Civil Rights is over, that *segregation* and *oppression* are words reserved for museum exhibits. As [Beverly D.] Tatum has argued, many White students in this country believe that race should no longer be considered an important factor in human relationships and that racial oppression is a thing of the past. We have certainly found such attitudes to be prevalent among our own White students. Indeed, the belief that there are no more wrongs to right— Michigan's constitution was recently amended to render Affirmative Action illegal—has been a serious impediment to students' understanding of Griffin's important work. . . .

Black Like Me in the Classroom

We recently had the opportunity to team-teach in a highly homogeneous, rural community—Hudsonville High School's student body is nearly 100 percent White. However, when we surveyed the students in our junior-level literature course, we found that over ninety-five percent of them either agreed or strongly agreed with this statement, "Hudsonville is a very diverse community." Unfortunately, many of our students fit the profile Tatum describes. During discussions of literature and current events, they frequently expressed their belief that "color shouldn't matter any more." Although they acknowledged the United States' painful, racist past, they were convinced that "that's over now." Like many of us, they found it difficult to "get behind the eyes" of people who might be different from themselves in important ways; they struggled to understand the experiences of people of color and of other victims of oppression and discrimination.

We thought that reading *Black Like Me* with the students might help them to understand more of the impetus behind the Civil Rights movement and might also open a discussion about instances of oppression, racial and otherwise, in modern society—even in Hudsonville. Unfortunately, our team-teaching arrangement came to an end just before it was time to teach *Black Like Me*; so Jennifer, with Brian serving as a collegial sounding board and planning partner, introduced the book by providing some extensive frontloading activities focusing on intolerance and the plight of people of color in the middle of the twentieth century. Before we began to read *Black Like Me*, we explored historical instances of intolerance through poetry like "We Wear the Mask" by Paul Laurence Dunbar and through non-fictional texts like Lawrence Otis Graham's "The Black Table is Still There" and "I Have a Dream" by Martin Luther King, Jr. We also looked at and discussed the labels and stereotypes that many students in Hudsonville use to draw distinctions between cliques and groups within their own student body.

As we discussed and analyzed these works, students began to relate historical instances of intolerance that they were familiar with from history classes to the themes of racial intolerance evident in the texts. They talked about the Japanese internment camps in the North American West during World War II, discrimination against Jews throughout history, and the "Trail of Tears." Because students were making these important connections, Jennifer thought that the pre-reading exercises had done a good job of helping the students to retrieve the background knowledge they would need to understand Griffin's story. But when the class was about halfway through *Black Like Me*, Kristiana, one of the students, walked into class and announced, "This JHG dude doesn't know what he's talking about. He's a fake and a phony. He can't possibly know what it is like to be Black. He's just pretending."

Doubting Griffin's Account

Although there is truth in Kristiana's assessment—Jennifer had been careful to explain to the class that Griffin, a White man "in disguise," could at best approximate the experiences of people of color—Jennifer was shocked by Kristiana's blunt and harsh analysis of Griffin and his account. After all, even if we discount Griffin's personal experiences because of the "phoniness" of his disguise, can we discount the experiences of others, the instances of hatred and oppression he observed first hand? Didn't his experiences in disguise give him (at least) a somewhat more realistic view of the day-to-day lives of people of color in the South? Until Kristiana's emphatic announcement halfway through the text, she had seemed empathetic to the plight of the people Griffin highlighted in his account. When Jennifer asked her to explain what she meant, Kristiana indicated that, because of his disguise, Griffin was an unreliable reporter. She felt that because Griffin was really a white man in disguise, she could not trust that his report was typical of the kinds of discrimination that were reality to many people during that time. Evidently, she saw no connection between Griffin's account and real life, either the real life of the '60s or the real life of the twenty-first century.

Emergency measures were in order. Kristiana was an influential student who had rightly emphasized a potential problem with Griffin's account. Jennifer wanted Kristiana to be free to speak her mind and to encourage her insightful, independent thinking, but Jennifer certainly didn't want Kristiana to shut down the discussion or to provoke her classmates to dismiss the book out of hand. She also didn't want anybody to miss the truths Griffin had observed from his camouflaged position.

As discussion proceeded that day, however, Kristiana gained an audience and a following. Other students chimed in to say that the book was okay so far as history goes, but that

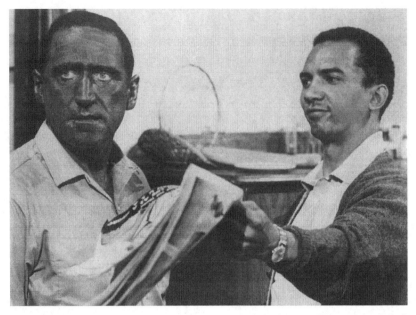

James Whitmore (left) and Al Freeman Jr. in a scene from the 1964 film version of Black Like Me. © Everett Collection.

racial discrimination had been "solved" when the Civil Rights Bill was signed. The more the students talked, the more confident Jennifer was that the kids were missing a very important piece of the puzzle: the connections between the kinds of oppression detailed in Griffin's story and the kinds of oppression found in modern society. But how can these connections be illuminated? One way is to do student-generated case studies.

Crafting Case Studies

In order to help the students see the relationships between the instances of discrimination and oppression in *Black Like Me* and the lives of modern-day citizens of Hudsonville, we decided to use case studies. Teachers in many disciplines, from law and medicine to information systems management to teacher education, have found that discipline-specific case analysis, "facilitates problem solving, decision-making, critical thinking, self-directed learning, self-evaluation, and interpersonal communications as well as the retrieval, access, and use of information" [according to Ann M. Tomey].

[Larry] Johannessen and [Elizabeth] Kahn note that case studies can be especially helpful for students of literature because a carefully crafted literary case:

> provides data to help them connect with [the character's] problem in the text and activates their prior knowledge so that they develop a deeper understanding of the issue the ... character confronts. It is designed to prepare students to think hard about the moral choices the [character] has to make in the novel and to get them to consider some of the consequences of having to make such a moral choice. . . .

We could have written a set of hypothetical cases dealing with real-world issues of oppression and discrimination, but we knew the students would connect in a deeper, more personal way if they had to think about real life in the world with which they were familiar. If they were going to forge connections between the text and their lives, we knew they would have to do some themselves. That was when our planning took an interesting turn. . . .

We wondered what might happen if we were to ask Jennifer's students to write their own cases as a way of responding to *Black Like Me* and as a way of convincing them that the book is really not so different from their own lives and experiences. The students' main criticism of the book was that it was "phony" or "unreal." We reasoned that if the students could write what they considered to be "realistic" case studies paralleling the situations Griffin records in his book, the students would be better able to see the ways in which the text could speak to modern-day Hudsonville—and they could no longer argue that they couldn't relate to the book.

Since the students had read over half of the text, they were familiar with the situations of discrimination and intolerance Griffin had observed and experienced. The plan was to have them reexamine a number of those specific situations and to write their own parallel case studies which included a similar type of intolerance, but in a setting more closely related to the students' own experiences.

One Classroom Strategy

The next day, when students entered the classroom, the desks had been rearranged; instead of being placed in rows, they faced each other in pairs. Between each set of desks was a lap-top computer, although our activity would have worked just as smoothly with paper and pencils. To introduce the collabo-rative case writing activity, Jennifer handed out the assign-ment page that outlined the requirements and their choices [as well as a model case study]. . . .

Together the class talked through the features of an effec-tive case study, focusing on the details that made the model case come to life. Jennifer emphasized the realistic nature of the details; if the features of the situation were at all improb-able, the entire case would lose its authenticity. Lastly, the class discussed the guiding questions for readers to consider and respond to at the end of each case. As a class, we decided that the guiding questions for our parallel cases would be: "What do you think this person should do next? How do you think this reaction will change the situation?"

With the model as a guide and their interest activated, the students began brainstorming a parallel situation to craft into an authentic case. The assignment page provided students with a list of scenarios and page numbers from *Black Like Me* to consider. Students could choose from situations in the text that ranged from a time when Griffin misinterpreted a white woman's sympathetic glance on a bus only to be spoken to harshly, to an incident when the White man at a custard stand directed an uncomfortable Griffin to an outhouse fourteen blocks away when relief was clearly visible on the property. In order to fulfill the assignment, each pair of students had to choose one situation from the text, brainstorm potential real-life scenarios together, and write a case that explored a type of discrimination or intolerance similar to that exhibited in their chosen scene.

The classroom came alive with conversation. Students began discussing experiences of their own with bullying, news headlines which focused on racial differences in the wake of September 11, emotional scars from elementary school playground traumas, brushes with homelessness, and methodical exclusion from social groups due to differences in appearance or socio-economic class. Their paired discussions were surprisingly, emotionally intense. They were listening to one another, they were providing suggestions to improve the cases, and they were connecting to one another even more deeply than Jennifer had hoped or anticipated.

Crafting the cases took all hour. Students eagerly revised and edited their cases, perhaps because they knew their classmates were going to be reading and discussing them. They added twists and details to ensure that each case did not have a clear-cut, "right" response, making the cases more authentic and more ethically challenging. They read aloud and compromised readily in order to make their cases the best they could be. Before they left for the day, they were to add the guiding questions to the end and be sure Jennifer had a printed copy of their case. They walked out the door discussing the ins and outs of the cases they had crafted, comparing with one another and already commenting on possible responses.

Students Grapple with the Task

The next day, Jennifer selected ten of the cases to photocopy on colored paper, assigning each case a different color. Jennifer was careful to include a variety of scenarios to help students recognize that the kinds of intolerance shown in *Black Like Me* are not confined to any one time period, geographic region, or societal arrangement. She was also careful to choose cases which did not overlap in setting or focus and which were "contentious" enough to provoke discussion. When students arrived on day two of the exercise, each received a case written by one pair of their classmates. They were instructed to read over the case and to respond in writing to the guiding questions at the end of the case. After about ten minutes of reading and writing, Jennifer instructed the students to trade with another classmate, making sure they didn't get the case they originally composed or the one they had just read. They read the new case and the response that one of their peers had just written, but this time they responded in writing by generating another, alternative way the characters of the case could react to the situation and discussing what might happen if they were to take this new course of action.

Normally, a handful of students respond to tasks such as these quickly and without much thought, hoping to carve out a bit of class time for a note to a friend or daydreaming, but that was not the case this time. These cases gave students the opportunity to share their own writing in a very real way with a very immediate audience. They were anxious to read what their peers had written and to hear what their colleagues had to say about their cases. . . .

Thinly Disguised Student Experiences

Matt and Kylee were an unlikely, collaborative pair during the writing stage. Kylee was successful in school and athletics, very popular. Matt suffered from some mental health challenges and often found himself on the outside of social groups. People generally avoided him because of his inappropriate outspokenness and frequent rants. Kylee and Matt never sat at the same lunch table at school and they were rarely at the same social events. They would not have worked with one another had they not been assigned to. As Jennifer observed their paired discussion from a distance, she was surprised to see the two of them speaking so earnestly to one another. Moving nearer, she noted that Kylee was listening intently to

Matt as he presented the outline for a potential case, and that Kylee freely shared her own views regarding his statements. They often turned the computer screen so that both of them could read and edit their evolving case. It was a true collaboration. The fruit of their cooperative efforts was a case which dealt with a young man who often found himself in rough waters—a barely concealed retelling of a situation from Matt's life. Together they wrote:

Imagine a place where you know you will not be safe, even though those in charge maintain that everyone has a right to be respected and valued in this place. Now imagine if this place were a part of your every day life. To most people, school is place to come to hang with friends and grow up confident, nurtured, and respected. Not for Miguel. Since he was a young child, Miguel struggled to make himself heard through his stuttering speech. He had many important things to say and contributions to make to every class, but often his speech overshadowed the validity of his thoughts and emotions. Because of the teasing and under-their-breath comments from his classmates, Miguel came across as angry and resentful. In class, if he was trying to convey his thoughts, he often changed his tone to stress the importance of his ideas. The other students in his classes took this as obstinance and a challenge. They didn't realize that he wanted to fit in with them more than anything. One day while Miguel tried to contribute to the discussion in World Studies, Luke began a barely-audible repetition of the stuttered words Miguel struggled to express. Other students joined in. The substitute teacher that day didn't quite know how to respond. Normally the others didn't have this opportunity to victimize Miguel so openly. By the time Miguel had completed one sentence, he was nearly in tears. He had important ideas to share; why couldn't his classmates be patient and compassionate? As Miguel left the room that day, Luke and his friends followed, mocking Miguel all the way down the hall.

> *What do you think Miguel should do next? What do you think*
> *will happen if he does this?*

When the class began to discuss this case, Matt was on the edge of his seat. He had first-hand knowledge of rough treatment from his peers. Jennifer watched the discussion unfold as many previously silent classmates shared that they disagreed with how some students treat others, and listened as those students asked aloud whether they were just as guilty if they did nothing to protect those who were treated poorly. The class eventually agreed that the way many of them had treated others (as perpetrators and as silent bystanders) was a part of the problem. Students were building bridges all across the room. Matt's perspective and experiences were finally honored by his classmates that day.

In several instances, like Matt and Kylee's, the stories on the page were all-too-true. But because the characters and situations in the cases were regarded as "made up," the students could speak from their hearts about the difficulty of the dilemmas without making themselves too vulnerable. . . .

Other, similarly personal cases gave rise to similarly intense discussions. Here's another example:

> Shaney Felop was an ordinary, 14-year-old girl living in Atlanta, Georgia. She loved her friends, family, and especially her computer. One day Shaney was innocently IM-ing her friends online when she received a strange IM from an unknown screen name. When she opened the message, a trembling welled up in the pit of her stomach. She knew exactly where it had come from. In her third hour geometry class, a group of five girls had begun teasing her about her less-than-designer wardrobe and constantly mocking her whenever she tried to participate in the class discussion. Recently she had stayed after class to talk with her teacher about why her grades were suddenly suffering a tailspin, hoping to have the opportunity to mention her stresses about the girls to him as well.

After thinking it over and receiving three subsequent IMs in the next hour, Shaney simply wrote three words in response: "LEAVE ME ALONE!" The next response she received chilled her to the bone. The girls' response told her that they were clearly taking this as seriously as she was. "Wait until tomorrow . . ." the response read. Shaney wasn't sure she would have the courage or the strength to face them in third hour tomorrow.

What do you think Shaney should do about the situation? What do you think will happen if she does this?

The Universality of Experience

When discussing this case involving harassment via technology, students heard the anguish in their classmates' crafted stories, which certainly hinted at reality for some who discussed with vigor and passion. What had once seemed a harmless form of teasing took on a much more dangerous aspect. Through their discussions, students heard how this kind of oppression, which might seem harmless to the teaser or could be viewed as typical teenage behavior, was perceived much differently by those on the other side of the teasing when students who had been victims of online harassment shared how it affected them. The students came to the mutual conclusion that this form of harassment is cruel and inappropriate, no matter the intent. And when they connected on-line harassment to the "hate stare" that Griffin and other Blacks endured in *Black Like Me*, students reconsidered the ways in which distant, supposedly impersonal cruelty can harm both victim and perpetrator. By modernizing the context and situation, students were able to better connect their lives to the life and experiences of John Howard Griffin, of the African Americans he lived among and wrote about, and of other victims of oppression throughout the world—even in Hudsonville.

As the discussion on the third day was winding down, Kristiana spoke again. She had been eerily quiet during the better part of the three days of discussion. She hadn't appeared to be disengaged, but she was clearly keeping her opinions and feelings private. She finally let the rest of us into her thoughts: "This is just like today! Even though we all are White and don't really have to deal with issues of color differences, we are just like JHG. History just keeps repeating itself over and over again." Kristiana was seeing that Griffin's experiences in the South related to her world today. It wasn't just about color barriers, but about the barriers all of us tend to erect between one another. She was able to use Griffin's text and the texts she and her classmates had created together to see her reality more clearly; and she wasn't the only one forging these kinds of connections. We were back to the book and it was finally hitting home for these students.

Though racism was not our primary focus as we discussed the kinds of injustice central to the students' case studies, we weren't in any way trying to minimize attention to race or distract students from issues of race—in fact, race remained a central topic of discussion. But we found that we couldn't get them into the discussion of race until we had gotten them to connect to other forms of injustice, especially from their own experiences. Because students came up with their own examples from what they knew of the world and their experiences, they were able to look more closely at the remainder of Griffin's work and see that his disguise did not prevent him from experiencing the harsh realities of racism. He was no longer labeled a "phony" or a "fake" in their eyes.

The Lingering Impact of the Case Studies

The use of student-generated case studies can create a rich forum for thoughtful discussion and can help students to build bridges between their own lives and the lives of seemingly distant and difficult literary texts. During our *Black Like Me* unit, our students engaged in creative conversation, negotiated and compared with one another in respectful ways, and valued one another's work and responses as we used their texts as the texts of our classroom. Because the strategy was so successful, we have used it at other grade levels with other texts and have found it to have similarly beneficial effects every time.

As successful as student-generated cases have been in our classrooms, we are just as excited about the ways in which the strategy seems to reap rewards in students' lives beyond the halls of our schools. These discussions don't just fall dead as students walk out of our doors; they are carried along and reverberate through their lives long after they graduate. Recently, almost four years after Kristiana graduated from high school, Jennifer had the pleasure of running into her in the local grocery store and then keeping in touch via e-mail over the course of the next several months. After learning that Kristiana was working her way through the decision whether to go to law school or enter the Teach For America program, Jennifer brought their conversation around to the lessons Kristiana might have learned through the time they spent together in that eleventh grade English class. Although Jennifer didn't mention *Black Like Me* in particular, Kristiana began her e-mail reply with:

> *Black Like Me*—ahhhhg! Well, where do I start!? Even though I still disagree completely with what Griffin did, I do think that the book could be used as a valuable resource. If there is debate and discussion about his actions, and students are able to formulate their own opinions of this man's decisions, it is a beneficial resource. This is what you pushed us to do, Mrs. H. You made us look at how we can influence our own world for the better by jumping off from Griffin's experiences and applying them to our own lives.

Other students have returned to tell us how our discussions of *Black Like Me* and the student-generated cases have influenced their views and changed their approaches to various situations as they have grown. Their reflections on our time together and their stories about the lasting results of our

Black Like Me unit are gratifying. From the beginning, we hoped that each of our students would begin to see John Howard Griffin, the African Americans he lived and wrote among, and each of our neighbors in Hudsonville (and beyond) as "human, like me." We are pleased to say that we have found exactly that to be the case.

CHAPTER 3

Contemporary
Perspectives on Race

Racism Is Internalized in Modern America

Nadra Kareem Nittle

Nadra Kareem Nittle is a journalist who has written about race, immigration, education, and civil rights for many publications, including the Los Angeles Times, El Paso Times, Santa Fe Reporter, L.A. Watts Times, *and the website* Racialicious. *She has headed the "Race Relations" section of About.com since 2010.*

In the following article Nittle discusses the dimensions of internalized racism. Nittle observes that cultural messages are extremely powerful and often persuade minorities to see things from the perspective of the majority, even when that is not in that minority group's best interests. Nittle specifically points out that, in the presence of clear and emphatically biased messages, members of minority groups may find themselves unconsciously adopting those views. This results in individuals who at once identify with their own ethno-racial subgroup and hold that group (including themselves) in poor regard.

Just what is internalized racism? One might describe it as a fancy term for a problem that's pretty easy to grasp. In a society where racial prejudice thrives in politics, communities, institutions and popular culture, it's difficult for racial minorities to avoid absorbing the racist messages that constantly bombard them. Thus, even people of color sometimes adopt a white supremacist mindset that results in self-hatred and hatred of their respective racial group. Minorities suffering from internalized racism, for example, may loathe the physical characteristics that make them racially distinct such as skin color, hair texture or eye shape. Others may stereotype those from their racial group and refuse to associate with them. And some may outright identify as white. Overall, minorities suffering from internalized racism buy into the notion that whites are superior to people of color. Think of it as Stockholm Syndrome[1] in the racial sphere.

The Causes of Internalized Racism

While some minorities grew up in diverse communities where racial differences were appreciated, others felt rejected due to their skin color. Being bullied because of ethnic background and encountering harmful messages about race in greater society may be all it takes to get a person of color to begin loathing themselves. For some minorities, the impetus to turn racism inward occurs when they see whites receiving privileges denied to people of color.

"I don't want to live in the back. Why do we always have to live in the back?" a fair-skinned black character named Sarah Jane asks in the 1959 film *Imitation of Life*. Sarah Jane ultimately decides to abandon her black mother and pass for white because she "wants to have a chance in life." She explains, "I don't want to have to come through back doors or feel lower than other people."

In the classic novel *Autobiography of an Ex-Colored Man*, the mixed-race protagonist first begins to experience internalized racism after he witnesses a white mob burn a black man alive. Rather than empathize with the victim, he chooses to identify with the mob. He explains:

> I understood that it was not discouragement, or fear, or search for a larger field of action and opportunity, that was driving me out of the Negro race. I knew that it was shame,

---

1. Stockholm syndrome is a psychological state noted in kidnapped persons and prisoners of war in which the captured person identifies with his or her captors even to the point of defending them and wanting to stay with them.

unbearable shame. Shame at being identified with a people that could with impunity be treated worse than animals.

Internalized Racism and Beauty

To live up to Western beauty standards, ethnic minorities suffering from internalized racism may attempt to alter their appearance to look more "white." For those of Asian descent, this could mean opting to have double eyelid surgery. For those of Jewish descent, this could mean having rhinoplasty. For African-Americans, this could mean chemically straightening one's hair and weaving in extensions. In addition, people of color from a variety of backgrounds use bleaching creams to lighten their skin.

It's important to note, however, that not all people of color who alter their physical appearance do so to look "whiter." For example, many black women say they straighten their hair to make it more manageable and not because they're ashamed of their heritage. Some people turn to bleaching creams to even out their skin tone and not because they're trying to uniformly lighten their skin.

Accusations of Internalized Racism

Over the years, a variety of derogatory terms have cropped up to describe those likely suffering from internalized racism. They include "Uncle Tom," "sellout," "pocho" or "whitewashed." Also, a number of nicknames for those suffering from internalized racism involve foods that are dark on the outside and light on the inside such as Oreo for blacks; Twinkie or banana for Asians; coconut for Latinos; or apple for Native Americans. Such name-calling is offensive and insults those who may not experience racial self-hatred but don't fit into a box.

While such name-calling is hurtful, it persists. So, who might be called such a name? Multiracial golfer Tiger Woods has been accused of being a "sellout" because he identifies as

"Cablinasian" rather than as black. Cablinasian is a name Woods devised to represent the fact that he has Caucasian, black, American Indian and Asian heritage.

Woods has not only been accused of suffering from internalized racism because of how he racially identifies but also because he's been romantically involved with a string of white women, including his Nordic wife [Elin Nordegren, a Swedish model, who divorced Woods in 2010 following public revelation of his infidelity]. Some people view this as a sign that he's uncomfortable with being an ethnic minority. Someone who refuses to date members of their own racial group may, in fact, suffer from internalized racism, but unless the person declares this to be true, it's best not to make any assumptions. In any case, children may be more likely to admit to suffering from internalized racism than adults. A child may openly yearn to be white, while an adult will likely keep such wishes to himself for fear of being judged.

Those who serially date whites or refuse to identify as an ethnic minority may be accused of suffering from internalized racism but so are people of color who espouse political beliefs considered detrimental to minorities. Conservative Supreme Court Justice Clarence Thomas and Ward Connerly, a Republican who's led the effort to strike down affirmative action in California and elsewhere, have been accused of being "Uncle Toms," or race traitors, due to their right-wing beliefs. Whites who associate mainly with people of color and politically assign themselves with minority groups have historically been accused of betraying their race as well. Whites active in the Civil Rights Movement were harassed and terrorized by other whites for seemingly "siding" with blacks.

Internalized Racism and Self-Esteem

It's impossible to tell if someone suffers from internalized racism simply based on their friends, romantic partners or political beliefs. But if you suspect that someone in your life suffers from internalized racism, try to talk with them about it. Ask them, for example, why they exclusively associate with whites, want to alter their physical appearance or downplay their racial background. Point out positives about their racial group and why they should be proud to be a person of color.

African American Children Still Suffer from a Negative Self-Image

Hazel Trice Edney

Hazel Trice Edney is a veteran journalist who for ten years served as editor in chief of the National Newspaper Publishers Association News Services. In 2010 Edney launched the Trice Edney News Wire, a syndication service carrying items of special interest to the approximately one thousand black-owned or black-oriented newspapers in the United States.

In the following selection Edney reports the findings of young filmmaker Kiri Davis. Noting how her high-school-aged friends often voiced frustrations as they struggled to resolve the inherent conflicts between media images of what constituted beauty and their own appearances, Davis chose to reenact the famous 1950 "doll test" of social researcher Kenneth Clark that was used by NAACP lawyer Thurgood Marshall to successfully demonstrate to the US Supreme Court how damaging school segregation was to young children. Despite more than half a century of progress in race relations, Davis found that almost exactly the same proportion of modern African American preschoolers preferred white dolls and called dark-skinned dolls "bad" or "ugly."

The reassuring female voice asks the child a question: "Can you show me the doll that looks bad?"

The child, a preschool-aged Black girl, quickly picks up and shows the Black doll over a White one that is identical in every respect except complexion.

"And why does that look bad?"

"Because she's Black," the little girl answers emphatically.

"And why is this the nice doll?" the voice continues.

"Because she's White."

"And can you give me the doll that looks like you?"

The little girl hesitates for a split second before handing over the Black doll that she has just designated as the uglier one.

A Startling Wake-Up Call

This was not the 1954 doll test used by pioneering psychologist Kenneth Clark to help make the case for desegregation in the landmark *Brown v. Board of Education* Supreme Court decision that outlawed segregated public schools. Rather, it was a doll test duplicated in Harlem, N.Y., last year [2005], more than a half-century after *Brown*. To the chagrin of parents and psychologists across the nation, the results were unchanged.

The test is again in the news because of an eight-minute documentary produced by 17-year-old film student Kiri Davis of Manhattan's Urban Academy who participates in the Reel Works Teen Filmmaking program, a free after-school program supported by cable network *HBO*.

The videotaped doll test resulted from a collection of writings Kiri had compiled on issues of importance to Black girls in her high school. In that writing, she noticed that complexion was a recurring theme.

"I knew what my friends were going through. These standards of beauty just kept coming up," she said in an interview with the *NNPA News Service*. "I thought it was an issue that needed to be exposed more, although at times it seemed too taboo to talk about. But I thought a film would just put it all out there and cause discussion."

The Original Doll Test of 1950

In realizing that so many dark-skinned girls have been told that lighter or Whiter skin is more beautiful, Kiri decided to drive home her point by conducting the doll study. The chil-

A seven-year-old girl shops for dolls at a store in Long Beach, California, 2011. In a test conducted in 2006, young African American children were given a white doll and a black doll and asked to choose the "nice one." Fifteen out of twenty-one chose the white doll. © Marmaduke St. John/Alamy.

dren are from a Harlem Day Care Center. And 15 of the 21 children surveyed preferred the White doll over the Black one.

Mr. Clark and his wife Mamie Phipps Clark, also a psychologist, conducted the doll study in 1950 that showed how racial segregation destroyed the self-esteem of Black children. The Clarendon County, S.C. experiment involved 16 Black children, ages 6 to 9. They asked the children their perception of a White doll and a Black doll. Eleven of the students said the Black doll looked "bad" and nine said the White doll looked "nice."

The test results influenced the U.S. Supreme Court to hold school segregation to be unconstitutional in the 1954 *Brown* case. Arguing against the "Separate but equal" doctrine in 1952, Thurgood Marshall, then an attorney for the NAACP Legal Defense and Educational Fund, cited Mr. Clark's work as proof of the doctrine's damage to the self-image of Black children. On May 17, 1954, Supreme Court Chief Justice Earl Warren announced the court's decision to desegregate schools in *Brown v. Board of Education.* Mr. Clark's doll test was one of his citations as proof of the psychological damage on Black children.

No Change in Self-Image

The Davis test shows that psychology has not changed very much at all.

"I'm really not shocked, I am sad to say," says Julia Hare, a San Francisco psychologist. "If you keep doing what you have always done, you're going to keep getting what you have always had. Our children are bombarded with images every day that they see on television screens and on coffee tables—either the light-skinned female that everybody is pushing or they give preference to the closest to White images."

Kiri's film also features brief interviews with four teens who object to having been stereotyped as less intelligent or uglier simply because they do not meet the expectations of advertisers' perceived standards of beauty.

That White-is-right image is also projected through music.

"Look at our rap artists and entertainers, and not just the Lil' Kims and the Beyoncés," opines Ms. Hare. "Their skin is getting lighter and lighter and they're getting blonder and blonder."

Gail Wyatt, professor of Clinical psychiatry at the University of California at Los Angeles, says she would recommend to any parent to instill racial pride into their children well before pre-school.

"Youngsters come into their homes making disparaging remarks about being brown or African-descended or about nappy hair," says Prof. Wyatt. "It is a definite concern of any parent. We want to know how our children can grow up in their own skin. We can't leave that part of a child's development to the school system or the neighborhood."

Instilling Racial Pride in Children

Children should be socialized between the ages of 2–4 to understand culture and skin color, Prof. Wyatt says. "They should be taught a concept of beauty and a context of ancestry."

Kiri's mother, Ursula Davis, an education consultant, says educating her daughter and instilling pride about her heritage was a high priority around the home.

She says that when Kiri was in pre-kindergarten, enjoying the tales of Cinderella and Snow White, she once said out loud at school that she wanted to be a princess, too. A little friend, a Latino boy, quickly dispelled her dream. He told her she couldn't be a princess because she was Black and that only White girls were princesses. For a while, Kiri believed her little friend—but not for long.

"She grew up with African art around her. We took her to an exhibit in the Smithsonian about Black women in Washington, D.C.," Ms. Davis recalls.

"She began to read voraciously about Black heritage and African American studies. She has immersed herself since she was very young and we have immersed her in the celebration of who she is."

And it has obviously paid off, as Kiri looks forward to a future in filmmaking that will also instill pride.

"I only want to make films that are about issues that are of importance to me, films that don't show the stereotypes," Kiri shares.

Hollywood's Role

Some parents say their children are bombarded with countless negative images each day and that it takes a special effort to compete with those images.

"I make sure I know what they see and what they watch on television. And many times, we are watching things together," says Alethea Holland, a Washington, D.C. mother of three daughters ages 7, 9 and 15. "And I give them each a mirror and I try to make them look in the mirror and appreciate their beauty and I make sure that they hear what I say; not what other people say, especially at school."

Sandra Cox, director of the Coalition of Mental Health Professionals in Los Angeles and a past president of the Association of Black Psychologists, says the short film clip may have understated the problem.

"I believe if any of us out here [on the West Coast] were to do the same study, it would be still worse," she says. "Hollywood created the standard."

Talking About Racism Is Awkward and Painful but Vitally Important

Jen Graves

Jen Graves is an educator and writer living in Seattle. She writes regularly for the Stranger, *a noted Seattle-based newspaper, and she has also contributed pieces to the* Believer, Newsday, *and* Arts in America.

Although Graves's argument in the following selection is grounded in conditions in and around Seattle—which is, according to the 2010 census, one of the "whitest" cities in the United States—her observations and findings ring true across the country. Even as Americans have become ever more sensitive to even mildly or accidentally racist utterances—and elected the first African American president—de facto segregation in housing, schooling, and the workforce has increased. Graves strongly suggests that "post–civil rights" America is badly in need of a vibrant antiracist movement involving conversation and consciousness-raising among whites.

One day in front of a class of art history students at Cornish College of the Arts, I say, "Raise your hand if you're a racist." I hadn't planned on this.

Understanding Your Own Biases

That class period I was focusing on James Baldwin and Glenn Ligon, both gay men, both African American, and it hit me that because there wasn't a black person in the room, things were getting abstract. This art is valuable and has to be taught—there really is no arguing against Baldwin, and Ligon's painting *Black Like Me #2* was one of the first President [Barack] Obama brought to the White House—but how do you teach someone to have a relationship to it?

So I throw it out there: Raise your hand if you're a racist.

As my students do that thing where they sort of just look at you, perplexed, I raise my own hand. I am deeply embarrassed, but I feel I have to be honest if I am asking them to be.

"You've never had a negative thought based on racial bias?" I ask.

Very slowly, arms begin to rise. I understand their confusion. Theirs is a generation in which we have elected a mixed-race president, but affirmative action has been struck down for being racist.

Redefining Racism

It was white Seattle parents (and a few from Kentucky, too) who fought all the way to the United States Supreme Court in 2007 so that race would be eliminated from consideration as a tiebreaker in competitions for placements in public schools. Despite the fact that racial inequities remain steady year after "post–civil rights" year—across indexes of health, wealth, and education—racial balancing, according to the 2007 ruling, is no longer a "compelling state interest."

The racial tiebreaker in Seattle was originally instituted to end de facto educational racial segregation. But now segregation across Seattle schools is worse than it was in the 1980s. A few years ago, the *Seattle Times* published mind-blowing maps of the data; this same backslide has happened around the country.

"The way to stop discrimination on the basis of race is to stop discriminating on the basis of race," declared US Supreme Court chief justice John G. Roberts Jr., in 2007, siding with the Seattle parents whose kids didn't get into Ballard High because they were white. This is legal color blindness. It has dubious precedent: In 1883, 18 years after the abolition of slavery, US Supreme Court justice Joseph P. Bradley wrote a majority opinion that ended reconciliation laws because former slaves must "cease to be the special favorite of the law."

Today the same argument is made under the precious neologism that laws intended to redress racial inequity are themselves racist. "Racist is the new n-----," says Riz Rollins, the writer, DJ, and KEX [radio] personality. "For white people, the only word that begins to approximate the emotional violence a person of color experiences being called a n----- from a white person is 'racist.' It's a trigger for white people that immediately conjures pain, anger, defensiveness—even for white people who are clearly racist. 'Racist' is now a conversation stopper almost like that device where you can skew a conversation by comparing someone to [Adolf] Hitler. It's an automatic slur. And only the sickest racists will own up to the description."

Pervasive Modern Segregation

White people in Seattle are more likely to own rather than rent. White people are more likely to have health insurance and a job. White people are more likely to live longer. White people are less likely to be homeless. White people are less likely to hit the poverty level. White people are less likely to be in jail. White kids are *nine times* less likely than African Americans to be suspended *from elementary school* (in high school, it's four times higher; in middle school, it's five times, according to the district's data). Nonwhite high-school graduation rates in Seattle are significantly below white graduation rates—even if you're Asian, regardless of income level.

And then there's the white Seattle police officer beating "the Mexican piss" out of a guy. The white Seattle police officer punching a 17-year-old African American girl in the face.

In this photo from February 7, 2012, Mark Porter looks at a controversial billboard to create awareness of the sometimes hidden "white privilege" that reduces opportunities for minorities in Duluth, Minnesota. Viewpoint author Jen Graves stresses the need for white people to talk about racism. © AP Images/Richard Tsong-Taatarii.

The Seattle Police Guild newspaper editorial that called race-and-social-justice training classes "the enemy," "socialist," and anti-American.

Not that racial experience is monolithic. It's not black and white. But it's *real*. And across all measurable strata, white people in Seattle have it better.

Yet nobody is racist.

The 2010 US Census data led to reports of Seattle being the fifth whitest city in the country—reinforcing the perception of this place as a white place. But if you look at the actual numbers, 66 percent of people in Seattle identify as white, which means that *one in three* people are not white. That's not a white city. It only seems like a white city when you're in, say [neighborhoods like], Ballard or Wallingford or Fremont. If you walk the street expecting every third person you see not to be white, well, then you'll see how weird it is to be in Ballard or Wallingford or Fremont, where almost everyone is white. If you walk the street in Rainier Valley, the opposite is true.

"In Seattle, there's really a small amount that you have to do to be labeled a hero of diversity," says Eddie Moore Jr., the Bush School's outgoing director of diversity, who describes Seattle as "a segregated pattern of existence."

He adds, "It's just that there's really no real challenge to how the structure in Seattle continues to assist whiteness and white male dominance in particular. When you say 'white supremacy' or 'white privilege' in Seattle, people still think you're talking about the Klan. There's really no skills being developed to shift the conversation. How can we be acknowledged to be so progressive, yet be identified to be so white? I wish that's the question more Seattleites were asking themselves." . . .

The Right Way to Address Racism

Every conversation about race is tortured—palpably awkward, loaded with triggers, marked by the blind spots of perception and presumption—but that doesn't mean you're doing it wrong or should stop doing it, says Scott Winn. That means you have to keep on.

"Once I realized I was racist, it was, well, what am I going to do about it?" says Winn, a mild-mannered white guy in his 30s. "That shifts the defensiveness."

Ten years ago, Winn cofounded CARW (you say "Car W"), or the Coalition of Anti-Racist Whites. For him, getting involved in antiracism "ultimately was not a moral shift but a strategic one." He already knew the world was racially-f---ed. He just had to figure out what to do next, and he began by examining whiteness as the invisible structure that defines everything—that needs to be explored and then exploded.

"Whiteness is the center that goes unnamed and unstudied, which is one way that keeps us as white folks centered, normal, that which everything else is compared to—like the way we name race only when we're talking about a person of color," Winn says. "We can name how some acts hurt people of color, but it's harder to talk about how they privilege white folks." . . .

After the first meeting I go to, I describe to CARW member Esther Handy my sense that this is a conversion experience, that everything around me has begun in recent years to look different, with a totality that feels spiritual—waking up to white privilege. (For me, embarrassingly, the real awakening began late, with a 2008 story about transracial adoptees that I wrote in *The Stranger*, and it continues, propelled selfishly by the fact that I am marrying into a family of color. I come late, and I mean to come humbly.) Gently bringing me down to earth and shifting the focus away from me, Handy says, "Our coming around to figuring out that we should be thinking about and talking about and doing work around racial justice is great and it can be spiritual, as you mentioned. But it is in service and in honor to the awesome organizations and leaders of people of color who have been doing this work for decades . . . The truth is that communities of color are thinking about racial justice all the time. They're living it and breathing it, and there's a group of white folks supporting that work, but it's only a small fraction of the white community at this point."

I ask her how to talk about racism with people who don't want to see it. I'm not talking about Tea Partyers; I'm talking about people like some of my friends and family, lefties who care, people who are on my team. Attempts to bring up race in editorial meetings at *The Stranger* have been as klutzy as anywhere. Even for perfectly decent, well-meaning, progressive people, it can be hard to see the connection between unintended acts of racism and actual racial injustice.

"I start with the facts," Handy says. "It's clear these injustices exist. I say I'm trying to understand the systems that create these inequities, and what's my role in working to change things. Reaching out and sharing these concepts with families and friends is absolutely part of the work, it's just not all of the work. Getting our racist uncle to stop saying bigoted things is not going to change the system. But we're not going to change the system without talking to our friends and family about it. While it benefits us not to talk about race, let's look at these disparities that just don't seem right."

I ask how often she encounters resistance to conversations about race among white people in Seattle who consider themselves progressive.

"I'd say every day," she says. "We're confused about it and we've been taught to be defensive about it. I don't think we should be too surprised about that."

Winn says, "Exposure is often the key thing that trips people into awareness." The old "black friend" routine. Yes, it helps to seek out friends who are racial minorities if you want to understand racial injustice. Yes, this is weird. But so is the history of judging people based on something as arbitrary as skin color; we have to work with what we've got.

A Growing Movement

"After that, I think many white people are integrationists in that 'beloved community' way, but integration usually means assimilation," Winn says. "As in, you've gotta act like us for this to work. So exposure *on the terms of people of color* is important. At CARW, we create a space that's not a PC [politically correct] space. If you say something that's not cool, we say here's why language matters. That talking about it is a skill." . . .

"The test of how racist you are is not how many people of color you can count as friends," I recall someone telling me—I can't remember who now. "It's how many white people you're willing to talk to about racism."

Through CARW, I find out about WEACT, or Work of European Americans as Cultural Teachers, a group of educators who give presentations on white antiracism in Seattle schools. The reception to these presentations varies widely depending on the school. Like, at Ballard High School, the reception tends to be disbelief and defensiveness (i.e., "What are you talking about?"), whereas at Franklin High School, students go, "Yeah, duh."

The antiracist white movement in Seattle is growing.

White Antiracists?!

If you're white and you tell a white friend you're going to a community meeting about zoning or bike lanes or homelessness, that seems normal—like you might even make a difference in your little way. But try saying you're going to a meeting of white antiracists. . . .

White people saving trees: check. Ending poverty: check. Improving racial equity: What's the catch? If you're white and talking about race, or working for the NAACP [National Association for the Advancement of Colored People], people will ask you to explain yourself.

Doing it isn't pretty. I've made a fool of myself. I've been accused of being a race traitor. A comment on a recent Slog post I wrote reads, "You've got some issues of your own, there, sweety, and it's not the first time you've used 'white' as a pejorative. Let go of just a tiny bit of your guilt complex, and you just might find that white people can be wonderful, too." . . .

Teaching Whites to Listen

The United States was started by white people, for white people. That's the premise of the White Privilege Conference, founded in 1999 by Eddie Moore Jr., the former Bush School diversity director quoted earlier. Today, the conference is held in a different city each year, and where it used to bring maybe a couple hundred people, now more than 1,500 attend.

"It is not a conference designed to attack, degrade, or beat up on white folks," its website reads.

"There's some pancakes I'm not gonna be able to flip over," Moore says. "But what I say up front is that what whiteness does, as a structure, is to limit your ability to listen to people of color, to hear people of color, to *believe* people of color. I would encourage people to embrace that as true, and then start to work through it—and to use me as a resource. I'm not trying to villainize anybody."

So one answer to the question *What can I do?* is simple: Listen. Believe.

"I had to stop talking to white people about race, because I kept getting retraumatized," an African American friend told me about her days as a diversity trainer. "They just wanted to talk about why they weren't racist."

As Moore argues, segregation—whether enforced or voluntary—teaches us to disbelieve racism. I grew up in a middle-class white suburban neighborhood. Although we never had a black family over for dinner, every house on our street hosted black men doing perp walks through our living rooms on the news. I didn't realize the contradiction until much later—that our seemingly all-white existence was predicated on keeping other people *other*.

Race Is Ever Present

"It's really important to recognize that race affects everything you do—and that to act otherwise is just naive," says Julie Nelson, the director of the Seattle Office for Civil Rights (she's white; her predecessor was an African American woman).

Every city has one of these Offices for Civil Rights, to deal with legal antidiscrimination claims, but Seattle has an additional arm of government (only two and a half full-time positions, but supported by a small army of volunteers) devoted to racial justice, called the Race and Social Justice Initiative (RSJI). It began in 2006—it was the first of its kind in the nation—in response to an anti–affirmative action initiative sponsored by Tim Eyman. (Thank you, Tim Eyman.)

At least in Seattle, racial balancing is a compelling goddamn state interest. The RSJI is officially anti-color-blind. Not finding a racially equal world, it does not pretend at one. The city worked around the fact that Eyman's initiative specifically disallowed "quotas" or "set asides"—rather, the city strengthened the conditions of eligibility for getting city contracts by using the terms that are allowed in order to do the same thing: "good faith efforts" and "aspirational goals." The result has been a rise in contracts to minority-owned firms. Based on statistics that show that racial minorities in Seattle are still less likely than whites to hold diplomas and college degrees, the RSJI worked to remove unnecessary degree requirements from city jobs, which earned the RSJI a mocking on the local Fox News (a sign you're doing a good job). The RSJI reaches into every department. It influenced Seattle City Light to change its streetlights policy, which used to be replaced on a call-and-complain basis—a system that works fine in affluent, native-English-speaking communities where people know to look on a light pole, call the provided number, and trust that the city will come out to fix the problem. Now streetlights are changed on a fixed rotation that begins in the South End.

None of this is perfect—and more people of color still work in lower-paying jobs in the city's own 10,000-strong workforce, Nelson says—but at least the City of Seattle acts like it recognizes the existence of racism.

The Benefits of Whiteness

Nelson's office high up in the municipal building is full—really, *full*—of paintings by the African American street artist Darryl, who for years has been sitting on corners throughout the city, selling his scrawled paintings on cardboard. They say things like "What in the hell WRONG with my ass." (My fiancé bought one that sits in our living room and reads, "100

YEARS OF BLUE MOONS.") I didn't imagine I'd see the phrase "What in the hell WRONG with my ass" scrawled across anyone's office in this tower high above the city, but the sound of Darryl's voice way up here emphasizes the distance down to the street.

What Nelson says is this: If you're white, you have to own it. None of this I'm-not- white, I'm-beyond-it-and-I'm-Norwegian stuff. White people have to see race according to the terms they actually benefit from. Not that whiteness is a monolith, any more than nonwhiteness is. As Mab Segrest writes: "Women are less white than men, gay people are less white than straight people, poor people less white than rich people, Jews than Christians, and so forth." But what might matter, what *should* matter, is that whiteness is a real force that you've personally benefited from in one way or another if you're white. . . .

[Seattle sculptor Sean] Johnson is half black, half white, and originally from Columbus, Ohio. He says Seattle's racism is unlike the racism anywhere else, because Seattleites act like they're above it.

"I've had a conversation [about privilege with someone] like once a week for a while now," Johnson says. "It's a denial that's almost more offensive than somebody just coming out and saying a racist word to us. I've been arguing about this in a bar and been thrown against the coals like I don't know what I'm talking about—that there's no way Seattle's racist, there's no way Seattle's segregated—yet I'm the only black person in the room. Yeah, it is."

He goes on, "I have this friend from Mississippi, and we were both saying that we've never encountered anything like it before. There's a collective thought that it's a progressive place, so that everything has been done to make things equal, and any form of 'No, it's not enough' is either greeted with passive-aggressiveness or 'No, you don't know what you're talking about.'"

Being Aware of Your Racial Lens

"Remember: Seattle doesn't have a race issue," Tali Hairston says, laughing, during a pause in a heated public conversation about race at Taproot Theatre in June [2011]. Hairston, a Rainier Valley native who directs Seattle Pacific University's John Perkins Center for Reconciliation, Leadership Training, and Community Development, is descended from white plantation owners and black slaves. His family was the subject of the 2000 book *The Hairstons: An American Family in Black and White*. . . .

"Your life story produces a racial filter," he explains in a conversation after the panel. "It might be a lens so thick that everything gets drawn into looking like it's about race, or so thin that when someone says something is racial, you go, oh hell no, it's not. As a white person, you have to own the development of your own racial lens. Because whether you're aware of it or not, you have one."

It reminds me of something said by the white man sitting on the other end of the panel, Ron Ruthruff, a close friend and neighbor of Hairston's.

Subtle Shades of Perception

"The number 7 bus tells me things about myself," Ruthruff had said.

"Seattle people, we are really nice on the outside," he said. "The problem, I would argue, is that many of the things we struggle with regarding race in Seattle are covert. What do I see? I'll be really honest. I see two school districts in Seattle, one in the north end, one in the south end. You know what kids in the community call Garfield [High School]? They call it the slave ship, because the white kids are on the top two floors and the black kids are on the bottom two floors. I see my son walk into a classroom with his [African American] best friend [Hairston's son], one receiving the benefit of the doubt, the other being questioned—same thing in a movie theater."

Ruthruff pointed over to Hairston, wearing a suit; Ruthruff wore jeans. "He can't wear jeans and get taken seriously," Ruthruff said. "Tali can't carry no plastic bag on an airplane. In our neighborhood, I'm affirmed for living in the Rainier Valley. Meanwhile, people look at Tali and say, 'You're still in the Rainier Valley? We thought you were moving on up.'" . . .

The End of White Affirmative Action

"Three hundred years of affirmative action for white people," is how author and activist Sharon Martinas sums up American history.

The original "whites"—well-bred, high-class people, not those dirty Irish or Italians—were based on someone's dim memory of the beauty of women from Georgia, on the Black Sea, historian Nell, Irvin Painter writes in her new book, *The History of White People*. (The word "Caucasian" might have been "Georgian," except that the German man who coined it knew there was an area called "Georgia" in the nascent United States, and didn't want to confuse people!) Layers of ridiculousness piled up, like a lie compounding. Science was pushed and pulled. Tomes full of charts and graphs demonstrate that the race scientist's most sophisticated tool for centuries was— wait for it—measuring human heads with a ruler. True.

African American scholar Cornel West suggested in 2008 that the somewhat more wounded, struggling Americans of the 2000s rather than the Americans of, say, the 1950s, are well-positioned to *feel* race. After 9/11, "for the first time in the whole nation, my fellow citizens had the blues across the board: they felt unsafe, unprotected, subject to random violence, hated for who they are. It's a new experience for a lot of Americans."

He continued, "It's a very American thing, in many ways, to be sentimental, to create your little world of make-believe, live in your bubble. And then sooner or later—like Wall Street—boom! Here comes reality. Boom, here comes history. Boom, here comes mortality."

Right around September 11 was when a handful of white people began the current movement of white antiracism in Seattle—and not too soon. I can't help but think that in many ways, the natural white allies for the needed next generation of racial justice work—progressives who still may not have heard of CARW or antiracism—are instead unwittingly playing into the hands of race-baiting right-wingers simply by remaining silent.

Worsening Segregation

"Diversity, at least in the short run, seems to bring out the turtle in all of us," Rich Benjamin writes in his 2009 book *Searching for Whitopia*, in which he spent a year in the growing, increasingly white neighborhoods that are creepily cropping up all over the country. A 2008 study from the Pew Research Center showed that racial segregation in this country is worse than income-level segregation.

Is Seattle in danger of becoming a whitopia? The largest swaths of racial minorities are now living far north and far south, keeping racial separations alive, for various reasons, economic and otherwise. In some ways, we don't seem to *want* to live in racially mixed neighborhoods. Instead, we consume polarizing simplifications. In May [2011], a study by Harvard and Tufts researchers made headlines around the world. The study was called "Whites See Racism as a Zero-Sum Game That They Are Now Losing," and came to the stunning conclusion that white people believe they are the real victims of contemporary racism (reverse racism). But look closer at the study—it surveyed 417 people *total*. You can fit more people than that on some buses. The sample was not even close to statistically significant. Yet like the idea of Seattle as a "white city," word about it spread fast.

"Our racial thinking needs a truly twenty-first-century upgrade," Benjamin writes. "Identity politics is letting America down, on the one hand. Race and structural racism still matter, on the other."

"Rather than thoughtfully discussing race," he writes, "Americans love to reduce racial politics to feelings and etiquette. It's the personal and dramatic aspects of race that obsess us, not the deeply rooted and currently active political inequalities. That's our predicament: Racial debate, in public and private, is trapped in the sinkhole of therapeutics."

There's a riddle at the heart of our racial lives, he writes: "It's common to have racism without racists." He means the redneck, *Deliverance*-style kind—easy to identify, easy to marginalize.

How else to explain a generation of people who voted for Obama, and who cried tears of happiness at what his election meant, but are doing nothing to eliminate racial inequality where we live?

"Awash in its racial conundrum, America has delightful people who are perfectly comfortable with widening segregation and yawning socioeconomic inequality that often breaks along racial lines," Benjamin writes. "Let's call that a problem."

American Public Education Still Fails Students of Color

RiShawn Biddle

RiShawn Biddle is the editor and publisher of Dropout Nation, *a leading blog focused on reforming the American public education system. Biddle's award-winning editorials have appeared in the* American Spectator, *among other publications, and he has served as education policy adviser to the National Council on Teacher Quality and other organizations.*

In the following selection Biddle raises several recent instances of public school teachers and administrators openly berating their students of color and characterizing these children as "future criminals" and "dirty, nasty, bad." Although the most prominent national news items tend to highlight white teachers, Biddle points out that African American teachers and administrators are equally guilty of such prejudice. He concludes that these stark instances of racial bias demonstrate fundamental weaknesses in the teacher-training system that undermine the effectiveness of the American education system, regardless of the race of the child or teacher.

This week's [August 2011] news that Paterson, N.J., teacher Jennifer O'Brien was suspended from her job after declaring earlier this year that she was merely a "warden for future criminals" (instead of her actual role as a first-grade teacher), has led to discussions about the need for more black and Latino teachers—especially men—in America's teaching corps. Commentator Dr. Boyce Watkins, in particular, declared in a piece for *NewsOne* that the lack of diversity in the teaching corps has led to "Black/brown inner city children poisoned by the white female teacher from the suburbs". The solution, argues Watkins, is to recruit the "thousands of highly-qualified Black and brown teachers, consultants and counselors who know how to handle Black children."

A Lack of Diversity and Sensitivity

Certainly, Watkins is right that we need more minorities in the teaching profession, and just as importantly, we need more men in the teaching ranks. Women make up 79 percent of the nation's teachers and most of them are white. This lack of diversity in the teaching ranks has helped contribute to a major problem in education: The lack of role models, especially men of all races and backgrounds, who can serve as powerful examples of achievement for our children. Young men of all ages need strong male role models. And young black men, half of whom will likely drop out of high school before they reach senior year of high school after a decade of educational neglect and malpractice, need them most of all.

Yet Watkins fails to consider that there are plenty of examples of black teachers and leaders who think just as lowly of black children (and kids of other backgrounds). Consider Jersey City Superintendent Charles Epps, who was chastised by *Dropout Nation* and others earlier this year for declaring that the young women attending the traditional public schools there were "our worst enemy" in his (abysmal) effort to improve education in the district, and that many of the kids in the district's schools were "dirty, nasty, bad". Then there are the even worse examples of low expectations for black children in districts such as Indianapolis Public Schools and Detroit's woeful school system, where blacks control the central offices, hold principal jobs, serve as school board members and make up large percentages of the teaching corps. That some of the best-performing schools and districts in America for black and Latino children include charter school outfits founded by white men such as the Knowledge Is Power Program and Green Dot, along with the fact that some of the most-important reform efforts that are helping black children succeed are also being led by whites, also proves false the notion that only black teachers and leaders can serve black children.

Preparing Teachers for Suburbia

If anything, there are plenty of black teachers and black principals who care just as little for the educational, economic and social futures of black children as those of other races. This shouldn't be surprising. As University of Wisconsin-Milwaukee points out, most of the nation's university schools of education are geared toward preparing teachers to work in suburbia and with white students, failing to prepare them for urban backgrounds and to work with black, Latino and Asian children, no matter their economic background. Given that most black teachers and principals are educated in those same schools—and come from middle class backgrounds having little experience dealing with poor children—it isn't shocking that many of them may be just as ill-equipped to teach black kids, especially those from poor households, as their white and Latino peers. There are plenty of black teachers and leaders like Epps who could use some courses in cultural competency.

There is also the problem that far too many teachers— along with others working in American public education— embrace the Poverty Myth of Education, that only some kids can learn, that children from poor and minority households are incapable of mastering anything more than rudimentary knowledge, and that their families deserve little more than disdain and pity. Even if they don't say it publicly, they privately believe this myth to be gospel—and it can't help but affect their teaching. Jean-Claude Brizard, the new head of Chicago Public Schools—where African-Americans make up 30 percent of all teachers and 40 percent of staff overall—hit upon that point yesterday during his presentation before the City Club of Chicago.

A Sign of Fundamental Failures

But empathy for children isn't the only part of being a high-quality teacher. They must also have strong subject knowledge competency, have strong instructional ability, be gifted as classroom leaders, should hold kids, adults and themselves to high expectations, and must be entrepreneurial self-starters who can take on classrooms no matter what they are. Right now, we don't have enough of these teachers, either for black children or for all kids. As the National Council on Teacher Quality pointed out last month [July 2011] in its latest report on teacher preparation, one out of every four ed schools didn't require their ed school students interning as student teachers to spend time with mentoring teachers to learn all the things full-time teachers must do (including engaging parents) once they leave for classrooms. Add in the fact that 54 percent of all teachers are trained at ed schools with low entrance re-quirements—along with the reality that few ed schools prop-erly train teachers in the science of teaching reading and mathematics—and it will be hard for even a caring, culturally competent teacher to provide high-quality instruction to any student, no matter their race or class.

The case of Jennifer O'Brien does exemplify the need for diversity in teaching staffs. It also shows the problems that black families have in securing high-quality education for our kids, even in relatively diverse suburban communities such as Fairfax County [Virginia, adjacent to the District of Colum-bia]. But, more importantly, it shows the need for improving how we recruit and train teachers in the first place. We need to select high-quality talents who care for children and also can do all the things teachers must do to help our kids suc-ceed. We must overhaul how we train teachers—even starting new alternative teacher training programs outside of ed schools—in order to get those teachers ready for every child and classroom. And we have to hold every teacher, principal and superintendent accountable for doing the best for all of our kids and especially black children.

Our kids deserve better than to be called criminals by laggard, uncaring teachers and leaders. They deserve a high-quality education fit for their futures.

An Unexpected Epilogue for Two Civil Rights Icons

David Margolick

David Margolick is a contributing editor at Vanity Fair *and a longtime contributor to the* New York Times Review of Books. *In his fifteen years as legal affairs reporter for the* New York Times, *Margolick was nominated for the Pulitzer Prize on four occasions.*

Elizabeth Eckford and Hazel Bryan—both high school students in 1957—appeared together in what became an iconic photograph from the civil rights era: Bryan sneers and hurls some racial epithet at Eckford, who is one of nine African American students stoically attempting to attend classes at the segregated Little Rock Central High School in Arkansas. In the following article, Margolick explores the unlikely experiences of these two women, who have served as the largely anonymous faces of racial hatred and quiet perseverance for more than fifty years.

Who *doesn't* know that face?

It's the face of a white girl—she was only 15 years old, but everyone always thinks her older than that, and judges her accordingly—shouting at an equally familiar, iconic figure: a sole black school girl dressed immaculately in white, her mournful and frightened eyes hidden behind sunglasses, clutching her books and walking stoically away from Little Rock Central High School on Sept. 4, 1957—the date when, in many ways, desegregation first hit the South where it hurt.

An Iconic Photo

It's all in that white girl's face, or so it has always appeared. In those raging eyes and clenched teeth is the hatred and contempt for an entire race, and the fury of a civilization fighting tenaciously to preserve its age-old, bigoted way of life. You know what the white girl's saying, but you can't print it all: commands to get out and go home—"home" being the place from which her forebears had been dragged in chains centuries earlier. That what that white girl was actually doing that day was more grabbing attention for herself than making any statement of deep conviction doesn't really matter. Of anyone with *that* face, you simply assume the worst. You also assume she is beyond redemption, especially if, symbolically, she is more useful as is than further understood or evolved.

So how is it that fifty-five years later, it is this same white girl—even more than the black girl—who feels aggrieved, who considers herself the victim of intolerance, who has retreated into embittered sadness? How can it be that she, who was so prominent at the joyous 40th anniversary of the events in Little Rock, celebrated by President Bill Clinton among many others, was invisible at the 50th, and ever since?

The black girl is Elizabeth Eckford of the Little Rock Nine. Moments earlier, she'd tried to enter Central High School, only to be repeatedly rebuffed by soldiers from the Arkansas National Guard placed there by Gov. Orval Faubus. A mob baying at her heels, Elizabeth is making her way, fearfully but determinately, toward what she hoped would be the relative safety of the bus stop a block away.

The face belongs to Hazel Bryan. Hazel, the daughter of a disabled war veteran, was largely apolitical, even on matters of race; while sharing the prejudices of her parents, she cared far more about dancing and dating. Being in that crowd that morning, making a ruckus, out-shouting all of her friends, was a way of getting noticed, and far more exciting than going

Hazel Bryan, right, shouts at fellow student Elizabeth Eckford as she arrives at the newly desegregated Little Rock Central High on the first day of school in 1957. © Everett Collection.

into class. She'd thought nothing would come of what she'd done, and nothing ever would have had she not been captured in mid-epithet by Will Counts, a young photographer for the *Arkansas Democrat*.

Struggles and Regrets

If anyone in the picture, which reverberated throughout the world that day and in history books ever since, should feel aggrieved, it's of course Elizabeth Eckford. What Counts had captured both symbolized and anticipated the ordeals that Elizabeth, a girl of unusual sensitivity and intelligence, would face in her lifetime. First came the hellish year she and other black students endured inside Central, and then decades in which the trauma from that experience, plus prejudice, poverty, family tragedy, and her own demons kept her from realizing her extraordinary potential.

With enormous courage and resiliency, Elizabeth ultimately made a life for herself and has largely come to peace with her past. Paradoxically, it's been Hazel, who has led a life of far greater financial and familial security, who now feels wounded and angry. Someone who once embodied racial intolerance feels victimized by another form of prejudice, in which good deeds go unappreciated, forgiveness cannot possibly be won, and public statements of contrition breed only resentment and ridicule.

Concerned over her sudden notoriety, only days after the infamous photograph appeared, Hazel's parents transferred her from Central to a rural high school closer to home. She never spent a day in school with the Little Rock Nine and played no part in the horrors to which administrators, either lax or actually sympathetic to a small group of segregationist troublemakers, allowed them to be subjected. And she left her new school at 17, got married, and began a family.

But Hazel Bryan Massery was curious, and reflective. Tuning in her primitive Philco [TV] with the rabbit ears her father had bought her, she heard the speeches of Dr. Martin Luther King Jr., and saw those black protesters getting hot coffee and ketchup poured on their heads at segregated lunch counters or being routed by fire hoses and German shepherds. Such scenes brought home to her the reality of racial hatred, and of her own small but conspicuous contribution to it. One day, she realized, her children would learn that that snarling girl in their history books was their mother. She realized she had an account to settle.

Transformation and Reconciliation

Sometime in 1962 or 1963—no cameras recorded the scene, and she didn't mark anything down—Hazel, sitting in the trailer in rural Little Rock in which she and her family now lived, picked up the Little Rock directory, and looked under "Eckford." Then, without telling her husband or pastor or anyone else, she dialed the number. Between sobs, she told Elizabeth that she was *that* girl, and how sorry she was. Elizabeth was gracious. The conversation lasted a minute, if that. In the South, in the '60s, how much more did a white girl and a black girl have to say to one another?

Still, Hazel never stopped thinking about the picture and making amends for it. She severed what had been her ironclad ties to an intolerant church. She taught mothering skills to unmarried black women, and took underprivileged black teenagers on field trips. She frequented the black history section at the local Barnes & Noble, buying books by Cornel West and Shelby Steele and the companion volume to *Eyes on the Prize*. She'd argue with her mother on racial topics, defending relatives who'd intermarried.

Secretly, Hazel always hoped some reporter would track her down and write about how she'd changed. But it didn't happen on its own, and she did nothing to make it happen. Instead, again and again, there was *the* picture. Anniversary after anniversary, Martin Luther King Day after Martin Luther King Day, Black History Month after Black History Month, it just kept popping up. The world of race relations was changing, but to the world, she never did.

Finally, on the 40th anniversary of Central's desegregation in 1997, Will Counts returned to Little Rock and arranged for

Elizabeth and Hazel to pose for him again. Hazel was thrilled, Elizabeth, curious. Their first meeting was predictably awkward, but the new picture, showing the two women smiling in front of Central, revealed only the barest hint of that. It all but took over the next day's *Arkansas Democrat-Gazette*, and very nearly upstaged President Clinton's speech the next day, in which he worked in a reference to them both. Soon, a poster-sized version of the picture was available: "Reconciliation," it said. Everyone rejoiced; Thanks to Elizabeth and Hazel, Little Rock, maligned for 40 years, bathed in instant absolution.

A Strained Friendship

Then, quietly, Elizabeth and Hazel discovered something quite miraculous: They actually liked each other. For all their differences—Elizabeth was better-read, Hazel's life far better-balanced—they shared a good deal. Both were introspective, skeptical, a bit isolated; neither fit in anywhere, including in their own families. They visited one another's homes, took trips together, spoke to schools and civic groups. In the process, Hazel helped pull Elizabeth out of her shell, then to blossom. Unemployed, on mental health disability for years, Elizabeth soon returned to work, as a probation officer for a local judge. Two years after they'd first met, the pair even appeared on *Oprah*.

[Oprah] Winfrey hadn't bothered hiding her incredulity, even disdain, that day: Of all people, *these two* were now friends? But as rude as both felt her to have been, she'd been on to something. The improbable relationship had already begun to unravel.

A student of, and stickler for, history, Elizabeth looked for—and, she thought, spotted—holes in Hazel's story. How, for instance, could Hazel have undertaken something so cruel so casually, then remembered so little about it afterward? And why, after all these years, did she absolve her parents from any blame? At their joint appearances, Elizabeth could treat Hazel impatiently, peremptorily. Meantime, others in the Little Rock Nine either shunned Hazel or complained of her presence at various commemorations.

But resentment came as well from whites, particularly whites who'd attended Central, particularly those from better families, who'd thought that, even by always looking the other way, they'd done absolutely nothing wrong during those dark days and, truth be told, considered Hazel and her ilk "white trash." Forty years earlier she'd given them all a black eye; now, she was back, more conspicuous, and embarrassing, than ever. At a reunion she foolishly, or naively, attended, she felt their cold shoulder, and could hear their snickers. None of *them* had ever apologized for anything they'd done or not done, and, as far as Hazel could tell, they'd been none the worse for their silence.

A Lingering Longing to Connect

Ultimately, it grew too much for Hazel. She cut off ties with Elizabeth—for her, Sept. 11, 2011 marked another anniversary: 10 years had passed since they'd last spoken—and stopped making public appearances with her. Her interviews with me—granted only with great reluctance—will, she says, be her last. When I asked the two women to pose together one last time (Elizabeth turned 70 last Tuesday [in October 2011]; Hazel will in January [2012]) Elizabeth agreed; Hazel would not. Hazel was poised to vote for Obama in 2008; after all, even her own mother did. But so deep was her hurt that she found some excuse not to.

So the famous photograph of 1957 takes on additional meaning: the continuing chasm between the races and the great difficulty, even among people of good will, to pull off real racial reconciliation. But shuttling back and forth between them, I could see that for all their harsh words—over the past decade, they've only dug in their heels—they still missed one another. Each, I noticed, teared up at references to the other. Perhaps, when no one is looking—or taking any pictures— they'll yet come together again. And if they can, maybe, so too, can we.

For Further Discussion

1. Most Americans are certain that they can tell white people from black people—often insisting they can do so simply by hearing a voice. Knowing what you do about John Howard Griffin's experience, do you think this is the case? Is race easily identified? If not, why not? If so, how do you explain the 2008 complaints from African American activists and pundits that then-candidate Barack Obama "wasn't black enough"—specifically because he was born of a white mother and an African (not African American) father?

2. After his experiment, Griffin often referred to himself as "black" or "formerly black" (although Griffin readily acknowledged that his experience was very limited and by no means gave him anything approaching the insight that any African American might offer). In his selection, Robert Bonazzi argues that for the course of his experience Griffin was, without a doubt, black, fully sharing in the daily (if not life-long) struggles of African Americans of the late 1950s. Conversely, many writers have criticized Griffin's experience as shallow to the point of meaninglessness. Long after he returned to being "white," Griffin was threatened and severely beaten by organized racists (such as the KKK). In your opinion, was Griffin black for the duration of his experiment? Was he still black even after he'd allowed his skin to return to its normal pigmentation? Finally, what does it mean to be African American? Explain your answers.

3. Why is *Black Like Me* so compelling? Many readers, reviewers, and critics have voiced puzzlement over the book's enduring popularity, characterizing the writing it-

self as over-written and melodramatic. According to Hugh Rank, Griffin's book is appealing to readers because of how well-structured the argument is. Nelson Hathcock builds on this, pointing out that Griffin's tale of racial passing through "enemy territory" is a foundational "spy story" that continues to be popular for the same reason that the James Bond franchise (begun at around the same time) continues to flourish. Is *Black Like Me* interesting because of its message of racial injustice, or because of the thrill of Griffin's predicament and his "secret"? Explain.

4. Following the 2008 election of Barack Obama—the first African American US president—many commentators declared that the United States had "moved past race." The findings detailed by teachers Jennifer Haberling and Brian White, as well as selections such as the one by David Margolick, tend to indicate that Americans have progressed toward greater compassion and racial understanding. But the 2006 restaging of the infamous 1950s "Doll Test" (demonstrating internalized racism among very young African American children, and reported in Hazel Trice Edney's selection) argues otherwise. Observations made by Jen Graves on antiracist activism in the Pacific Northwest in 2009 likewise seem to indicate little progress in American race relations. While there is no denying that race relations have greatly improved in the last half-century, how much have they improved? How can we measure this improvement? Is "ignoring race" possible, or even desirable? Explain your answers.

5. Griffin says he embarked on what he called his "journey into shame" in order to explore the *real* experiences of African Americans living under Jim Crow and to faithfully report these back to the white majority (who often believed that conditions "weren't that bad"). This would seem like a very selfless endeavor. Nonetheless, many readers and critics have argued that Griffin's experiment in

racial passing was self-serving, and although risky, proved to be an excellent way for a "mediocre novelist" to gain international fame and build his career. Do you believe Griffin was altruistic or calculating in his experiment? Was this a stunt, or an enduringly important political action? Cite from the selections in your answers.

For Further Reading

Daniel Bradford and John Howard Griffin, *The John Howard Griffin Reader*, 1968.

John Howard Griffin, *The Church and the Black Man*, 1969.

———, *The Devil Rides Outside*, 1952.

———, *Prison of Culture: Beyond "Black Like Me,"* 2011.

———, *Scattered Shadows: A Memoir of Blindness and Vision*, 2004.

Grace Halsell, *Bessie Yellowhair: Journal of a White Woman Who Lived Among the Navajos*, 1973.

———, *In Their Shoes*, 1996.

———, *Soul Sister*, 1999.

James Weldon Johnson, *The Autobiography of an Ex-colored Man*, 1927.

Norman Mailer, *White Negro*, 1967.

Beverly Daniel Tatum, *Why Are All the Black Kids Sitting Together in the Cafeteria? A Psychologist Explains the Development of Racial Identity*, 2003.

Tim Wise, *White Like Me: Reflections on Race from a Privileged Son*, 2011.

Bibliography

Books

Robert Bonazzi   *Man in the Mirror: John Howard Griffin and the Story of "Black Like Me."* Maryknoll, NY: Orbis Books, 1997.

Baz Dreisinger   *Near Black: White-to-Black Passing in American Culture.* Amherst: University of Massachusetts Press, 2008.

Gerald Early   *Lure and Loathing: Essays on Race, Identity, and the Ambivalence of Assimilation.* New York: Penguin, 1994.

Frantz Fanon   *Black Skin, White Masks.* New York: Grove Press, 2008.

David Margolick   *Elizabeth and Hazel: Two Women of Little Rock.* New Haven, CT: Yale University Press, 2011.

Jonathan Metzl   *The Protest Psychosis: How Schizophrenia Became a Black Disease.* Boston: Beacon Press, 2011.

Dorothy Roberts   *Fatal Invention: How Science, Politics, and Big Business Re-create Race in the Twenty-First Century.* New York: New Press, 2011.

Greg Tate

Everything but the Burden: What White People Are Taking from Black Culture. New York: Broadway Books, 2003.

Gayle Wald

Crossing the Line: Racial Passing in Twentieth-Century U.S. Literature and Culture. Durham, NC: Duke University Press, 2000.

Harriet A. Washington

Medical Apartheid: The Dark History of Medical Experimentation on Black Americans from Colonial Times to the Present. New York: Anchor Books, 2008.

Tim Wise

Colorblind: The Rise of Post-racial Politics and the Retreat from Racial Equity. San Francisco: City Lights, 2010.

Periodicals and Internet Sources

Kristen Allen

"Anti-racism Groups Slam *Black Like Me* Film," *The Local: Germany's News in English*, October 22, 2009. www.thelocal.de.

Helena Andrews

"Pregnant Teen Like Me," *Root*, April 29, 2011. www.theroot.com.

Robin Caldwell

"Black Like Me? The Missing Faces in Technology and Innovation," *Huffington Post*, September 21, 2009. www.huffingtonpost.com.

Kevin Connolly   "Exposing the Colour of Prejudice,"
BBC News, October 25, 2009.
http://news.bbc.co.uk.

Cameron Duodu   "Our Son: Overnight, Obama Has
Ensured That the Situation in the
World Should Change Dramatically,"
New African, February 2009.

Kimberly Foster   "Black Like Me: When Being
'Light-Skinned' Isn't a Privilege," *For
Harriet* (blog), October 14, 2010.
www.forharriet.com.

Don Graham   "White Like Me," *Texas Monthly*,
August 2004.

Ms. H   "Black, Like Me: Teaching About
Race in a White Community,"
Universe as Text, June 8, 2011.
www.universeastext.com.

Priscilla Hart   "White Like Me—or, Seeing the
World Through *Black Like Me*,"
Christian Science Monitor, November
4, 2011. www.csmonitor.com.

Nicholas Lemann   "Crossing the Color Line," *Atlantic*,
February 1993.

Timothy K. Lewis   "Black Like Me: Is Racism Poisoning
Our Political Debate?," *Constitution
Daily* (blog), October 12, 2011.
http://blog.constitutioncenter.org.

Rachelle Linner | "Catholic Like Me: Known Primarily for His 1960s Bestseller *Black Like Me*, Catholic Convert John Howard Griffin Also Offers Spiritual Wisdom and Moral Insights That Are Still Waiting to Be Discovered," *U.S. Catholic*, November 2004.

Michele Martin | "African-American Images: The New Doll Test," *Talk of the Nation* (broadcast transcript), National Public Radio, October 2, 2006. www.npr.org.

Donald Reid | "Passings That Pass in America: Crossing Over and Coming Back to Tell About It," *History Teacher*, August 2007. www.history cooperative.org.

Cyprian Lamar Rowe | "Man in the Mirror: John Howard Griffin and the Story of *Black Like Me*," *National Catholic Reporter*, November 21, 1997.

Martha Southgate | "Writers Like Me," *New York Times Book Review*, July 1, 2007.

Urban Politico (blog) | "Black Like Me: Vol. 1," May 13, 2009. www.theurbanpolitico.com.

Urban Politico | "Black Like Me Vol. 2: Society's Bi-racial Conundrum," February 9, 2010. www.theurbanpolitico.com.

Bruce Watson | "*Black Like Me*, 50 Years Later," *Smithsonian*, October 2011. www.smithsonianmag.com.

Index